VOLVO

HAYNES CLASSIC MAKES SERIES

VOLVO

SAFETY WITH STYLE

RICHARD DREDGE

First published in November 2003

A catalogue record for this book is available from the British Library

ISBN 1 85960 964 3

Library of Congress catalog card no. 2003104832

Published by Haynes Publishing, Sparkford,
Yeovil, Somerset, BA22 7JJ, UK

Tel: 01963 442030 Fax: 01963 440001
Int. tel: +44 1963 442030 Int. fax: +44 1963 440001
E-mail: sales@haynes.co.uk
Website: www.haynes.co.uk

Haynes North America, Inc.,
861 Lawrence Drive, Newbury Park,
California 91320, USA

Page-built by Glad Stockdale
Printed and bound in England by J. H. Haynes & Co. Ltd, Sparkford

Note on imperial/metric conversions

Unless usually referred to only in metric units (eg engine capacity in cubic centimetres [cc] or litres [l]) or imperial units (eg carburettors in inches [in]), common measurements of length, area, volume, weight and speed in the text and specifications are given in imperial units with metric equivalents in parentheses, except in the following less common instances:

Fuel consumption: 282 ÷ miles per gallon (mpg) = litres per 100 kilometres (l/100km)
Torque: pounds-force feet (lb ft) x 0.113 = Newton metres (Nm)
Pressure: pounds-force per square inch (psi) x 6.895 = Kilopascals (kPa)

contents

Volvo
introduction

It was in 1924 that Assar Gabrielsson and Gustaf Larson first discussed the possibility of setting up a company to manufacture cars. In that year just, 15,000 cars found buyers in Sweden, and of those, only one in 20 was sourced from outside North America, so it made sense to design and build a car that was not only better-suited to Sweden's poorly surfaced roads, but was more durable.

In the early days, before the company even had a name, Gabrielsson and Larson were working just two evenings a week to get the ball rolling. They retained their full-time jobs and worked in Larson's home to produce a set of designs

with which they could tout for enough capital to go into limited production with a simple and rugged four-cylinder car.

The person commissioned to design the first cars was Helmer MasOlle, a landscape and portrait artist who had a fascination with cars. His own car was a 1914 Voisin, a make noted for its innovation, and from the outset, MasOlle decided that his first design for the new company would share something of this approach. Meanwhile, Larson had enlisted the help of a young engineer called Jan Smith, who acted on a consultancy basis to ensure these designs were as practical as possible. Although Larson had a great eye for detail there would be no harm in having a second opinion to analyse the designs he was producing.

In 1925, the company took on its first employee, a 23-year-old man named Henry Westerberg, although at that stage the Volvo name had not been adopted. His job was to help complete the drawings for the first batch of prototypes.

Coachbuilder Freyschuss of Stockholm was commissioned to produce the first ten bodies, nine of which would be open tourers, with the final one being a closed four-door saloon. By June 1926 the first running prototype was complete and ready for testing, and by the spring of 1927 the first batch of production cars would have to be ready. The deadline was met, as on 14 April 1927 the first car was driven off the production line of Volvo's Lundby factory. Apart from the fact

The two founders of Volvo, Gustaf Larson (left) and Assar Gabrielsson, initially ran Volvo in their spare time, around full-time jobs.

that the car moved off in reverse, because the rear axle had been assembled incorrectly, all had gone to plan. Now Volvo had to go out and sell some cars.

On offer was the OV4 (*OppenVagn* or Open Car, four cylinders) and PV4 (*PersonVagn* or Passenger Car, four cylinders), both powered by a 28bhp 1,944cc engine mated to a three-speed manual gearbox. The tourer

cost SKr4,800 (around £270 or $1,300) while the saloon was SKr1,000 more. Of the first 1,000 bodies, it was planned that half would be open tourers and the other closed saloons, but the problem was that Volvo chose to build the tourers first, and bearing in mind Sweden's climate, most potential buyers wanted something giving more protection from the elements.

The first Volvo was the OV4 open-top car, which did not prove popular because of Sweden's harsh winters.

As a result, for the eight months of production in 1928, just 297 cars were built, the majority of which were open tourers. It was clear that the focus had to be on the PV4 instead, so although the OV4 was listed until 1929, in the event, just 205 were made.

Assar Gabrielsson

It was thanks to Assar Gabrielsson's business acumen that Volvo thrived – in the early days the company could easily have faltered.

Born in Korsberga, in southern Sweden, on 13 August 1891, Assar Gabrielsson was 20 years old when he graduated from the Stockholm School of Economics. Having been one of the first-year intake of the new course, he and his tutors were legends of their time and Gabrielsson did incredibly well with his academic studies. He gained top marks in English, Russian and economics – skills that were to prove invaluable when he set up Volvo with Gustaf Larson.

In 1916, he joined one of Sweden's largest industrial empires, Svenska Kullagerfabriken (SKF), where he went on – at the age of 32 – to become sales manager for the entire group. While there he came to know about Gustaf Larson and his great skills as an engineer, so while Larson set about sorting out the engineering for the new car-producing company they were trying to establish, Gabrielsson ensured that the sums added up.

The venture soon became a great success, with Volvo going from strength to strength throughout Gabrielsson's time as managing director of the company. Although Larson's considerable engineering talents were of course key to the company's success, if it had not been for Gabrielsson's banking connections the capital to set up the enterprise simply would not have been there.

Assar Gabrielsson retired in 1956 but continued as Chairman of the Volvo board for another six years, until his death on 28 May 1962.

It soon became evident that the lightweight chassis used in the construction of the OV4 was not up to the job of supporting the saloon body of the PV4, the extra weight of which caused the lightweight chassis to flex, leading to the bodyshell cracking. A stiffer, timber-framed body therefore had to be designed and built in a hurry. By the start of 1928 the company was struggling to make any headway, with profits a long way off, and potential buyers not warming to the car, so the only option was to redesign the car substantially later that year.

Even at this early stage, Gustaf Larson had set down the strategy that Volvo would follow – a high level of quality would always be more important than a low selling price. So, instead of cutting back on the quality of engineering or of the materials used in its cars, Volvo would strive towards building cars which their owners could rely on. It is since the 1950s that the quality with which Volvo is most often associated

is for producing safe cars, but Volvo was actively promoting safety as far back as 1936. In its sales manuals (reputedly written by Assar Gabrielsson), which were given to all Volvo salesmen, and first produced in 1936, the references to safety are absolutely clear:

'An automobile conveys and is driven by people. The fundamental principle of all design work is, and must be, safety. Each individual supporting part and component in the car must be dimensioned in such a way that it will withstand all forms of stresses and strains which it can be expected to be subjected to, apart from collisions and similar types of impact. This applies chiefly to all supporting and driving parts.'

Although safety is designed in from the outset in any 21st century car, in the 1950s and '60s it was very much an afterthought for most car makers, but not so Volvo, which was presented with its first safety award in December 1962. The award was given to Gunnar Engellau by the Danish Road Safety

Board in recognition of the company's work in developing the seatbelt – despite the fact that cars with seat-belts were, at that time, considered to be more difficult to sell than those without! The first patent for a seatbelt had been filed in 1907, but it was not until the early 1950s that the idea began to be developed. By 1958 Volvo had its first three-point seatbelt patented and ready for production, although it wasn't until the following year that Swedish-market examples of the Amazon and PV544 were fitted with it as standard. From 1963, all Volvos were fitted with front seatbelts as standard but it was 1986 before a three-point seatbelt was available for occupants sitting in the middle of the rear seat; Volvo started fitting these as standard from 1990 – beating everyone else to it.

Soon after production started, the design of the PV4 was modified so that the car looked more graceful.

Gustaf Larson

Gustaf Larson was born in Vintrosa on 8 July 1887, and was one of eight children. By the time he was 24 years old he had moved to Coventry to work for engine manufacturers White & Poppe, having had a fascination for automotive engineering since an early age. He was briefed with helping to design a new engine for Morris but within two years of arriving in England he had returned to Sweden where he studied the internal combustion engine at Stockholm's Royal Institute of Technology.

Larson graduated in 1917, which was the year he joined SKF, where he first met Assar Gabrielsson, but it was not until 1924 that they started to make plans to establish a new car manufacturer for Sweden. It was while he had been in England that Larson came up with the idea of building a car from parts manufactured by outside suppliers, and one of his principles was that it was cheaper to do the job properly the first time rather than skimp on design or manufacture and then have to do it again. As a result, his perfectionism earned him a lot of respect throughout the car industry – one of his skills was to be able to identify weaknesses in design instantly, before progressing to the manufacturing stage, something that helped to reinforce Volvo's reputation for quality from the outset.

In July 1952, Larson retired, having been in charge of the company's technical development until then, but he continued to be a board member until 1958 and he acted as a consultant to the company until his death on 4 July 1968.

Gustaf Larson was the engineer whose methodical approach to manufacturing ensured that Volvo soon gained a reputation for quality.

In 1967, Volvo presented the results of Sweden's biggest ever traffic accident survey. Looking at 28,700 accidents involving 42,318 occupants, the survey showed how important wearing a seatbelt was. Passengers had survived impacts of 60mph (96kph) while others had been killed at speeds as low as 12mph (19kph) because they had not been belted in. As a result, Volvo began fitting seatbelts for rear-seat passengers from 1967, and in the same year, the rear-facing child safety seat was introduced for buyers of the new 144. This was a far cry from modern seats which are so simple to fit, the early seats required fiddly dismantling and reassembly of the front seats to get everything in place, but it was still an advance that nobody else offered. From 1968, head restraints were fitted as standard to the front seats of all Volvo cars to reduce the likelihood of whiplash injuries, while inertia reel seatbelts became standard on all Volvos from 1969.

The early 1970s marked the start of an obsession with car safety throughout the motor industry, in the wake of Ralph Nader's safety crusade and the publication of his book U*nsafe at any speed*. Safety cars were the order of the day with all the major car makers building test beds that would allow them to produce safer cars for the road. Volvo was no exception, building its VESC (see Chapter 8), elements of which would filter down into the company's production cars.

By 1972, Volvo was fitting a seatbelt reminder in all its cars, which was the first time that such equipment was offered as standard. Sensors in the front seats detected whether or not anybody was sitting there when the ignition was switched on and if there was a passenger but the seatbelt was not being used a flashing light indicated this. In the same year, Volvo introduced inertia seatbelts for rear-seat passengers, along with child door locks and the rear-facing child seat.

Nils Bohlin worked on safety within the aircraft industry, and in 1958 he patented the three-point seatbelt on behalf of Volvo.

Although Volvo had offered seatbelts as an option from 1957, the first three-point seatbelt became standard on all Volvo cars from 1959.

The first child seats might have been cumbersome to use, but they were at least available. No other car maker was working on such projects at that time.

The first Volvos used a four-cylinder side-valve engine, which delivered 28bhp from 1,940cc.

The influential American National Highway Traffic Safety Administration (NHTSA) carried out a series of crash tests in 1976, the result of which was the use of Volvo's designs as the standard which all other cars would have to meet. The NHTSA bought two dozen 240s which were crashed, the results were logged and it was these tests which allowed the standards for future crash testing to be drawn up. In the same year, Volvo's efforts towards making its cars safer had been recognised in Britain with the awarding of the Don Safety Trophy – the most prestigious road safety award available.

Then, in 1991, came perhaps the most significant safety development for many years, with the introduction of SIPS, Volvo's patented Side Impact Protection System. Rather more than mere side impact bars, this innovation was developed for the 850 and combined intelligent design that maximised the strength of the passenger cell with a means of dissipating the forces generated by a side impact through the car's structure. This meant reduced deformation of the monocoque, ensuring passengers were less likely to be injured by panel intrusion. By 1995, the SIPS concept had been expanded to include side airbags as well – driver and passenger dash-mounted airbags were by now expected on executive cars, so the race was on to find extra positions to mount airbags to reduce injuries further. Within three years of the introduction of the 850, Volvo had won no fewer than 35 awards around the world, most of them relating to SIPS.

Animated crash test dummy Clive Alive was the star of a film produced by Volvo to highlight road safety issues.

Why the Volvo name and logo?

The Volvo trademark first appeared on cars with tall, narrow grilles. In the wider, lower grilles since then, the symbol is still instantly recognisable.

The company which made the initial investment that allowed Gabrielsson and Larson to commence series production of cars was the same one which employed them both: SKF. This industrial giant was known first and foremost for its design and manufacture of bearings, and in 1915, had registered the name AB Volvo, but had not used it.

Volvo is Latin for 'I roll', a reference to the fact that bearings are known for their rolling properties. As SKF helped to find premises for car production as well as providing SKr200,000 to start production, it was only natural that the company would have a hand in coming up with a name for the fledgling car maker. As a result, Larson's company was allowed to use the name registered by his backer, but until they offered the name he was set to put his own surname on the cars' badges.

The logo chosen for the car was a diagonal line incorporating a circle which enclosed a diagonal facing arrow. This is the Swedish symbol for iron, known as the Mars symbol. The diagonal line itself was not supposed to become a design theme, but the Mars symbol had to be affixed to the radiator in some way. The stripe that was used to locate the trademark logo has probably become a more powerful symbol of Volvo than the logo itself.

These three Amazons are being suspended by a single piece of seatbelt webbing, to demonstrate the material's strength.

Bi-Fuel System (CNG, Biogas)

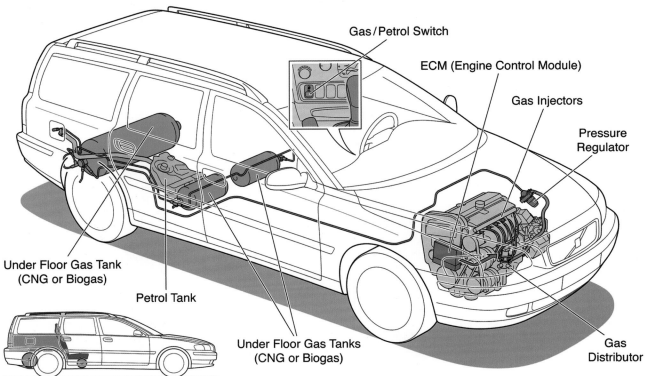

Gas/Petrol Switch

ECM (Engine Control Module)

Gas Injectors

Pressure Regulator

Under Floor Gas Tank (CNG or Biogas)

Petrol Tank

Under Floor Gas Tanks (CNG or Biogas)

Gas Distributor

Volvo V70

Because no after-market conversions take place, Volvo can guarantee the safety of its bi-fuel cars.

The other overriding quality associated with Volvo is that of environmental awareness. Although environmentalism was a bandwagon that relatively few car makers jumped onto until the 1980s – or even until the 1990s in many cases – Volvo realised much earlier than this that protecting the environment was something that would become increasingly important in all areas of manufacturing.

Volvo had already demonstrated its commitment to the environment by the end of the 1960s by looking at the impact its manufacturing plants had on their immediate surroundings. In 1970 the company was asked to

take part in a film called *Environment 70*. Made for European Environment Conservation Year in 1971, Volvo was chosen because of its work in emissions control, which had largely been prompted by American legislation.

When the UN Environment Conference took place in Stockholm in 1972, it was only natural that Volvo would do something to mark the occasion. The result was Volvo's first environmental declaration, drawn up by Pehr Gyllenhammar and which stated that the car should not be seen as something to be used at all costs – but with an important part to play in mobilising society, its benefits shouldn't be underestimated as it had become an indispensable means of transport. The key word in the declaration was 'responsibility' – something which Volvo had

promoted for many years, whether it was in a safety context or in an environmental one.

When legislation was passed throughout much of America dictating vehicle emissions would have to be drastically reduced, some car makers protested loudly and claimed the targets could not be met – at least not with their cars remaining affordable. The most ambitious state was California, which decreed that by 1977, emissions would have to be reduced dramatically – as a result, some manufacturers reckoned they would have to shut up shop because the targets were not achievable. Volvo however, proved everybody wrong with the introduction of the lambdasond in 1977. This allowed exhaust emissions to be cut by 90 per cent thanks to the use of a three-way catalyst working in conjunction with an oxygen-sensing control box. It was not long before all US-market Volvos had this system, but it could not be fitted to cars for use outside of America because of an unwillingness on the part of the fuel companies to sell unleaded petrol as lead damages the catalytic converter.

But Volvo wasn't just doing its bit for the environment by building cleaner running cars – producing its cars more cleanly was also important. By 1981, Volvo was addressing the emissions produced by its main factory at Torslanda, switching to water-based paints in place of the solvent-based chemicals previously used as well as reducing, by more than half, the energy used in some of the production processes within the factory. Despite Volvo's efforts to prove itself environmentally aware, it came in for a lot of criticism during

Volvo is one of the few car makers to offer bi-fuel versions of all its cars, each vehicle being built on Volvo's own production lines.

the 1980s, with environmental groups claiming that the company had no regard for the damage it was doing to the atmosphere. So, in 1986, the company employed an environmental auditor to report on how green the company was regarding its factories around the world, and to make sure that when any new legislation was introduced, Volvo was already in compliance.

Several years before catalytic converters became the norm for new European cars, Volvo introduced retro-fit systems in 1988 which could be fitted to cars built as far back as 1975 – a move helped by the fact that the company had not built many different models between the two dates. A year later, all plastic parts used in the construction of Volvo cars were being marked ready for recycling – again, a move that pre-empted other car makers by many years. By the mid-1990s, all Volvo cars would be free of asbestos, CFC and mercury, which ensured the annual environmental audits would return results that were ahead of

just about any other car maker in the world.

By the end of the 20th century, recyclability had become one of the most frequently used buzzwords. Not only did consumer goods have to be able to be recycled in the future, but items which had already reached the end of their useful lives were seen as the raw materials from which to build new products, rather than just starting again with virgin materials. Whereas more than 90 per cent of a car was constructed of metal (usually steel) in the 1970s, by 2001 this had been reduced to an average of just 76 per cent – the difference being because far more car components were now constructed of plastics. Such a move allowed Volvo to claim that between 95 and 98 per cent of the metal in its cars was capable of being recycled, and with 13 million cars a year being scrapped, such a figure was seen as essential in maintaining sustainability within the car manufacturing industry.

Acknowledgements

Although many people helped me research this book, there are two in particular who went well beyond the call of duty. The first is Tony Barrett of South Service Volvo in London. He specialises in keeping cherished (and not so cherished) Volvos on the road and helped check the manuscript for accuracy. I'm sure he breathed a heavy sigh of relief when I finally told him the chapters were going to press and he was off the hook!

Similarly, although everyone in the Volvo UK press office was very helpful, it was Sarah Atkins who saved the day on more than one occasion with her constant supply of press releases and photographs. Again, I'm sure Sarah was glad to see the book finished, despite the fact that she was impossibly good-natured about the steady stream of requests that flowed from my computer to hers.

The pre-war *Volvos*

By 1929 it was clear that the four-cylinder cars were underpowered, especially considering their high price. Even before the first OV4 had been built, Gustaf Larson was considering a six-cylinder car following a report made by Ivan Ornberg, an engineer friend. Ornberg held a senior post with American car maker Hupmobile, and when he returned to Sweden in 1931

he joined Volvo. Larson had requested that Ornberg look at Volvo's prospects when the company was first launched, and one of his recommendations was the production of a six-cylinder car. Although when the OV4 was introduced the American car makers were building cars with just four-cylinder engines, it was only a couple of years before they generally moved over to six – at least

The PV651 was Volvo's first six-cylinder car, which went on to inspire a line of large cars from the company throughout the 1930s.

OV4 and PV4
1927–1929

ENGINE:
Four cylinders in-line, iron block and head
Bore x stroke   75mm x 110mm
Capacity   1,944cc
Valvegear   Side-valve
Compression ratio   4.9:1
Fuelling   Single Solex
                       carburettor
Maximum power   28bhp (SAE) at
                       2,000rpm

TRANSMISSION:
Rear-wheel-drive; Three-speed manual

SUSPENSION:
Front: Leaf springs
Rear: Leaf springs with live
                       rear axle

BRAKES:
Front: None fitted
Rear: Drum
Mechanically operated
(Rear brakes were optional from 1928)

WHEELS:
20in wooden artillery wheels with 29 x
4.75in tyres

BODYWORK:
Separate chassis with open tourer (OV4) or
closed saloon (PV4) bodystyles

DIMENSIONS:
Wheelbase   8ft 8in (2.95m)
Track   4ft 3in (1.3m)

PERFORMANCE (Source: Volvo):
Max speed   56mph approx.

PRICE INCLUDING TAX WHEN NEW (1927):
OV4   SKr4,800
PV4   SKr5,800

NUMBER MADE:
OV4   302, including 27 bare
                       chassis and 70 pick-ups
PV4   691

PV651
1929–1930

ENGINE:
Six cylinders in-line, iron block and head
Bore x stroke   76.2mm x 110mm
Capacity   3,010cc
Valvegear   Side-valve
Compression ratio   5.1:1
Fuelling   Solex or Nife single
                       carburettor
Maximum power   55bhp (SAE) at 3,000rpm

TRANSMISSION:
Rear-wheel-drive; Four-speed

SUSPENSION:
Front: Half-elliptic leaf springs with hydraulic
dampers

Rear: Half-elliptic leaf springs with hydraulic
dampers

BRAKES:
Front & Rear: Drum
Mechanically operated (although final cars were
hydraulic)

WHEELS/TYRES:
Wooden artillery wheels

BODYWORK:
Separate chassis with open tourer body

DIMENSIONS:
Wheelbase   8ft 8in (2.95m)
Track   4ft 8in (1.42m)

WEIGHT: 3,300lb (1,500kg)

PERFORMANCE (Source: Volvo):
Max speed   60mph approx.

PRICE WHEN NEW (1929): SKr6,900

NUMBER MADE:
PV650–PV652 – 2,282; PV653 – 230
PV654 – 361; PV655 – 62

Notes:
The PV651 was superseded by the PV652 in
1930 with minimal changes. Later, an enlarged
engine displacing 3,266cc was fitted to the
PV652 which gave way to the PV653, PV654
and finally, the PV655 in 1933.

---

as an option to sit alongside the smaller offerings. As Volvo was competing with the major American car producers, this meant there had to at least be the option of a six-cylinder engine. Unlike the American car makers where the larger engines were seen as an option to sell alongside the smaller ones, Volvo's six-cylinder powerplants superseded the four-cylinder ones. Throughout the 1930s, all Volvos had these bigger engines and it was not until after the war, when the PV444 was launched, that there was a return to four-cylinder power for any of the company's products.

The first car to use this larger, more powerful engine was the PV651, which was launched in April 1929 and was based on the type PV650 chassis. Its 3,010cc six-cylinder side-valve engine, badged the DB, had nearly double the power of its predecessor, with 55bhp on offer. Although the exterior design of the new car marked a clear advance over the PV4, the trans-Atlantic influences were clear. It also remained resolutely conservative, to remain appealing to the middle-class buyers at whom the car was aimed. An increase in wheelbase meant the car was more comfortable to travel in

and a wider track allowed wider bodies to be built, increasing passenger space. The car also had brakes fitted to all four wheels and a hypoid bevel final drive – something which few other car makers had started to fit by that time. The big news though was the new engine, which allowed Volvo to take on the US manufacturers, at least in the company's home market.

At that stage, exports were still something for the future and when the Wall Street Crash happened in 1929 it was not the easiest of times for Volvo, which had chosen just the wrong time to move upmarket. While car sales continued at a slower pace than had been hoped for, Volvo moved into profitability thanks to the popularity of its trucks – especially once the six-cylinder engine had become available for use in these. Despite the reputation of the cars for reliability, their staid design and conservative engineering encouraged buyers to spend their money on cheaper American cars which were reliable enough for most people. Indeed, by the mid-1930s only one in 14 new car buyers was choosing a Volvo, the other 13 invariably choosing something from across the Atlantic. This added up to around 1,000 sales a year for the company, so, to increase its market share significantly, the company had either to add more cars to its range or make its existing

Bespoke seven-seater versions of the PV series were offered to taxi drivers, the new cars being badged as the TR series.

Identification of early Volvos

Three different prefixes were used for the identification of early cars – OV, PV and TR. The OV (for *OpenVagn*) and PV (for *PersonVagn*) were vehicles intended for private use. The difference between them is that the OV is an open car while the PV is a closed one. The TR is the odd one out, being intended for commercial use, and with TR

standing for *TrafikVagn* – Swedish for taxi.

Although the first six-cylinder car is sometimes referred to as the Type PV650, the first six-cylinder car to be produced by Volvo was the PV651. This is because the PV650 was just the rolling chassis upon which various cars, including taxis, were based.

cars more affordable. The decision was taken to go the former route.

As Volvo already had a reputation for reliability, it was felt that it made sense to play on this strength by targeting Sweden's taxi drivers with specially made cars that would suit their needs better than the standard PV651. By targeting taxi drivers, Volvo felt that it could increase market share significantly, so instead of

just producing a single version, urban and rural taxi drivers were to get their own derivatives. Both types had a longer wheelbase than the PV651 on which they were based and there was the choice of TR L (the Swedish acronym for Rural Taxi, but later renamed TR671) or TR S (for Urban Taxi, later the TR672) with a glass partition between driver and passengers. A longer

The PV654 was a more-rounded version of its predecessors, although it was still seen as very conservative.

That's why police forces and car hire companies were soon driving Volvos – something which could only reflect well on the company's products.

Although the cars were to prove popular, they were already lagging behind their (mainly American) competitors which were often equipped with hydraulic brakes all round. Volvo was still using mechanical brakes on all four wheels, so the change to a hydraulic system for the launch of the PV652 in 1930 could not come soon enough. The new car also featured an interior that was more luxuriously trimmed and equipped. Instead of replacing the PV651, the new car sold alongside it and although car production continued at just a trickle, at least Volvo was profitable. SKF had hoped that by the end of the 1920s there would be 8,000 vehicles rolling off Volvo's production lines each year, but in 1930 fewer than 2,000 vehicles were produced, most of which were trucks.

wheelbase gave space for seven seats and there was stronger rear suspension along with the option of a more luxurious interior. But it wasn't only taxi drivers which were targeted by Volvo – any group that had a high profile was fair game as the company tried to break into the fleet market.

The Carioca of 1936 wasn't staid in its design, but Volvo buyers had conservative tastes and the car was unpopular.

The Carioca's rear-wheel spats were considered too ostentatious for the typical Volvo buyer.

But overall, things were not going badly and by 1931, Volvo was on a roll. Its trucks were incredibly popular, taxi ranks were full of cars bearing the Mars logo and its cars had a name for ruggedness which meant buyers were opting for a Volvo in place of competing marques.

One of the reasons for the car's popularity was the attention to detail in the manufacturing process. Because only small numbers of cars were being built, the factory workers could afford to devote a lot of time and attention to each one. There was even a nine-man 'adjusting department' on hand to inspect each chassis and give it a test run both before and after the bodywork had been fitted. Having already been bench-tested by Pentaverken, Volvo's engine supplier, before it had even left the factory, each powerplant would be fired up from cold once installed in the chassis. The bare chassis would then be run on a tortuous 12-mile (19km) route and the engine tested when up to temperature. Once the body had been fitted the whole process would be repeated, so if anything was amiss the rigorous testing would highlight it before the car reached the customer.

In autumn 1933, the PV653 and PV654 arrived. They replaced the PV651 and PV652, with the PV654 having the higher specification of the two cars. The changes were not great, the biggest being a stiffer chassis. There were also wire wheels in place of the wooden ones fitted previously and the 65bhp 3,266cc engine, first seen in the PV652 in 1931, was standard for both cars. The greatest change however, was in the bodyshell, which was completely new, although it was still very conservatively styled and based on a wooden frame.

Although the cars were well built and able to compete on equal terms with their competitors, sales slumped. This was the period of the Great Depression and all manufacturing industries were feeling the pinch – and makers of luxury cars more so than most. As a result, fewer than 600 of the PV653 and PV654 were built before the last of the conservatively styled pre-war cars went on sale, the PV658 and PV659. Once again the higher number denoted a more luxurious specification and although the bodywork was similar to that on the cars they replaced, the new models featured a couple of significant differences – for the first time there was a radiator grille and a larger engine was produced for the new models.

Rated at 84bhp, the new power-plant was a bored-out version of the six-cylinder engine seen in previous Volvos, and now displaced 3,670cc.

As a result of sales barely picking up throughout the early 1930s, Volvo decided to come up with something more radical – the PV36, nicknamed Carioca after a popular dance of the period. This was inspired by Chrysler's daring Airflow, launched in 1934 and subsequently to prove a flop. It did not fail because it was a bad car or outdated underneath its aerodynamic skin, but simply because people thought it was ugly. When other stylists jumped on the aerodynamic bandwagon, they were not to know that such cars would be shunned, so that is why, when Volvo ended up producing its own sleekly styled car, nobody wanted to buy it. Considering the Carioca went into production in 1935, it seemed rather short-sighted of Volvo, as after all, the Venus Bilo concept (see Chapter 8) had proved a resounding flop when shown as a concept in 1933, so to put something similar into production just two years later was

Volvo toned things down with the PV51, although the drophead version was very stylish.

either foolhardy or incredibly optimistic.

The car had come about because of the work of Ivan Ornberg, who had been drafted in by Assar Gabrielsson to improve Volvo's fortunes. Considering how autocratic both Larson and Gabrielsson were, the fact that Ornberg was allowed to work on a new prototype without their involvement was a measure of their esteem for him. It was not until a full-scale wooden model had been produced that they were allowed to see the direction that their company would be taking from the mid-1930s. Although the car was radically different from any Volvo that had gone before, Larson and Gabrielsson should not have been too surprised with what Ornberg came up with because he had come from Hupmobile, bringing with him many

of the styling themes that were then just appearing across the Atlantic. So, when Ornberg showed them a car which was strongly reminiscent of the De Soto and Chrysler unveiled the previous year, it should have been no surprise.

The PV36 was built mainly of steel, although it still had an opening in the roof which necessitated the use of leathercloth to cover it. Whereas the American cars which had inspired it were moving towards a unitary construction (although none of them used a true monocoque yet), the Volvo was still using a bodyshell mounted on a separate chassis. The front crossmember carried independent front suspension with coil springs and wishbones while at the rear, there were leaf springs and an anti-roll bar. The six-cylinder engine and transmission were

carried over from the TR series, and thanks to bench seats in the front and back, there was room for six people to travel in comfort. The aim was to produce an initial batch of 500 cars to see how popular they were – a decision which was to prove a good one as in the event they took a long time to sell. Buyers were not ready for a car with such advanced styling and it was not until well into 1938 that the last examples were sold.

In the year that the PV36 was put on sale, Volvo reached a major point in its evolution, for in 1935 it was first publicly quoted on the stock exchange. SKF felt that its baby, nearly

The PV51 and PV52 (pictured here) were the first cars Volvo built that were designed for mass production.

The PV60's design was very American, but the car was reliable, with its side-valve six-cylinder engine and tough construction.

The PV52's simple interior was a slightly more upmarket version of the PV51's.

a decade old, was capable of standing by itself despite the fact that output was still below that projected. It had been hoped to build 3,500 vehicles in that year, but just 3,079 were produced – just under half being cars. The answer to expansion plans lay in producing something smaller and cheaper, as the company's dealers were crying out for a car they could sell which would compete with the large numbers of Fords, Opels and DKWs which were now flooding the Swedish market. So alongside the PV36, Ivan Ornberg was set to work on designing a smaller car aimed at this market.

The answer to the dealers' prayers arrived at the end of 1936, in the form of the PV51. Less radical than the PV36 and significantly cheaper, the car was greeted with intense interest by the buying public, although Ornberg had died earlier in the year so he did not see the

car make its debut. The PV51 was still more expensive than its rivals, but the Volvo badge meant it was worth paying for the extra quality as at least people could now afford the car – something that had not often been the case with the PV36. The engine was the same as the Carioca's and the gearbox was a three-speed unit with synchromesh on second and third gears. Although the PV51 had much in common with previous Volvos there was one significant difference – this was the first time that a car had been produced by the company which was built entirely of sheet steel pressings.

To keep costs down, the interior was less plush than the Carioca's and with a weight of around 29.5cwt (1,500kg), performance was much better than with previous Volvos, thanks to the 85bhp engine. The car was so incredibly spartan however that many buyers were put off – Volvo had skimped to the point that there was only one windscreen wiper and only one of the four doors had an armrest. The answer lay in the PV52, introduced in the spring of 1937. This was nothing more than a PV51 with more generous equipment levels, but it did the trick as car sales for 1937 were nearly double those of the previous year – although of the 1,804 cars built, just 56 were sold outside Sweden. In March 1938, to try to appeal to even more buyers, Special versions of the PV51 and PV52 were launched, with the spare wheel mounted in the boot instead of on the boot lid.

To eke out the lives of the PV51 and PV52 in both standard and Special forms, they received minor facelifts and changes in name. So, in 1938, the PV53 arrived to replace the PV51 while the PV54 replaced the PV51 Special. The PV55 superseded the PV52 and to take over the PV52 Special's place in the pecking order there was the PV56. There was also a PV57 which was merely a rolling chassis for bespoke bodywork, but the whole series was only a stopgap anyway until the

arrival of a significantly new model, which was scheduled for launch in February 1940.

When war broke out between Great Britain and Germany in September 1939, this project was severely disrupted, even though Sweden remained neutral, but it was not put on hold altogether. Work continued on the car, with further prototypes being built in 1942 and 1943 ready for its introduction when the war was over. So when hostilities ended in 1945, the PV60 was ready to go on sale, although production did not begin until December 1946. That was more than two years after the car had first been shown, as when the PV444 made its debut in Stockholm in 1944, the PV60 had been exhibited alongside it. By the time the car reached the showroom, it was already out of date – but that was no surprise as the project had been started nearly a decade before.

Its styling was based very heavily on US designs, but American car makers had changed the look of their cars radically since the war. The car sold well however, with Volvo's traditionally conservative buyers not too concerned by the fact that their car did not look especially modern, with 3,006 finding buyers between 1946 and 1950. This may not appear to be many, but in the years of austerity which followed the Second World War it was good going – what a shame that the two-door version which had been proposed initially never progressed beyond the drawing board.

Under the skin, the car was just as old-fashioned, as it was powered by the familiar side-valve six-cylinder engine although this had received some development with a raised compression ratio, a vibration damper on the crankshaft, and slightly more power. There was now a three-speed gearbox with overdrive that engaged and disengaged automatically, while inside the car there was a column-mounted gearchange and instrumentation that looked as though it had been taken straight from a contemporary American model.

The 800 series

By the mid-1930s, Volvo's TR series of taxi cabs was starting to look decidedly dated, but taxi drivers still loved them because they were reliable, popular with customers and very comfortable – although they were expensive to buy.

So, in 1938, Volvo unveiled a successor to the TR-series in the shape of the 800 series. There was the PV801, which had a glass partition behind the driver while there was also the PV802, without a partition. These were built specifically as taxi cabs but there was also the PV810, which had a longer wheelbase (139in/3.53m against 132in/3.35m) and which was available as just a chassis on to which bespoke coachwork could be fitted. The final version of the quartet was launched in 1940, which was the chassis-only PV800, with the same wheelbase as the standard cars.

These cars were very different from those they replaced, with far more up-to-date styling including a V-shaped front which, at the time, was seen as very daring. The familiar 3,670cc six-cylinder engine was fitted along with a three-speed all-synchromesh gearbox. Both the PV801 and PV802 were equipped with eight seats, including a trio of jump seats.

Throughout the war the cars continued to be built in limited numbers, but in 1946, production was increased dramatically to keep up with demand. In 1947 the series was redesignated to become the PV821 (with partition) and PV822 (without partition) while the chassis only was now the PV823 and the longer wheelbase chassis was the PV824. Apart from a slightly more powerful (90bhp) version of the six-cylinder engine becoming available, any changes were very slight.

A strange blend of old and new, the 800 series was known as the 'Sow' on account of its rounded lines.

Then, in 1950, there were major changes introduced when the 'Sow' arrived. This was the nickname given to the 800 series once the PV444 front end had been grafted on to the rear of the 800 series to create something that looked decidedly modern from the front and distinctly old-fashioned from the rear. The standard taxi with partition became the PV831 in the process while the model without a partition became the PV832. Predictably enough, the PV833 was the chassis-only version and the long-wheelbase chassis only was renumbered as the PV834.

Although the cars were conceived initially as commercial models, which would be working for a living, normally as taxis, it soon became clear that there was a demand for a PV800-based car that was a bit more special. Therefore, in 1953, the PV831 Disponent (or Manager) was launched, with a more upmarket interior. This included a radio with extra speakers, plusher upholstery,

and extra fittings. On the outside there were whitewall tyres, twin foglamps and maroon or blue paintwork in place of the black which was all that was available for the standard cars.

Just as when the cars had first gone on sale before the war, the new models were to prove immensely popular. There was not really much that could touch the Volvo's blend of space, comfort and reliability, so it was no surprise that the car stayed in production up until 1957, by which time over 8,000 had been built. Even then, taxi drivers protested heavily about the car being discontinued, as Volvo had no plans to replace it with anything remotely comparable.

The PV444/5 *Duett and* PV544

Volvo's new car was seen as the perfect addition to any family.

By 1943, the management at Volvo were already looking to the end of the war, and the types of car which would become popular. It was clear that luxury cars would not only be unaffordable to most people, but the costs of producing them would be inordinately high. The answer was to produce something relatively small that was simple and rugged – and most of all affordable for Mr and Mrs Average.

A team of 40 designers and engineers was assigned to the project in May 1943, and a consultant by the name of Helmer Petterson was hired to oversee the

PV444

1947–1957

ENGINE:
Four cylinders in line, iron block and head
Bore x stroke: 75mm x 80mm
Capacity 1,414cc
Valvegear Overhead valve
Compression ratio 6.4:1 (later 7.8:1)
Fuelling Single Carter carburettor
Maximum power 40bhp (SAE) at 3,800rpm
Maximum torque 76lb ft at 3,000rpm

TRANSMISSION:
Rear-wheel drive
Three-speed with synchromesh on 2nd and 3rd gears
(Four-speed gearbox from 1957 for export cars)
Final drive ratio 4.56:1

SUSPENSION:
Front: Independent with coil springs, telescopic dampers, wishbones, anti-roll bar
Rear: Live axle, coil springs, telescopic dampers, torque arms and Panhard rod

STEERING:
Type Cam and lever
Turns lock-to-lock 3.25

BRAKES:
Front & Rear: Drums
No servo assistance

WHEELS/TYRES:
Disc wheels with 5.00 x 16in tyres

BODYWORK:
Form of construction Monocoque
Body types available Two-door saloon

DIMENSIONS:
Length 14ft 9in (4.50m)
Wheelbase 8ft 6in (2.59m)
Track 4ft 3in (1.30m)
Width 5ft 2in (1.57m)
Height 5ft 0in (1.52m)

PERFORMANCE:
(Source: *The Motor*)
Max speed 74mph
0–60mph 24.9sec
30–50mph in top 12.7sec
50–70mph in top 10.9sec

PRICE (MARCH 1950):
Two-door saloon SKr6,490 (£448)

NUMBER MADE (TOTAL): 196,004
A 11,804
AS 700
B 4,500
BS 3,000
C 3,500
CS 4,500
D 3,500
DS 5,500
E 14,350
ES 17,599
H/HS 29,046
K/KS 33,918
L/LS 64,087

PV544

(1958–1965)

As PV444 except:

ENGINE:
Bore x stroke 79.4mm x 80mm
Capacity 1,582cc

Compression ratio 8.2:1
Fuelling Twin SU carburettors
Maximum power 85bhp (SAE) at 5,500rpm
Maximum torque 87lb ft at 3,500rpm

TRANSMISSION:
Four-speed manual

WHEELS/TYRES:
Steel disc wheels with 5.90 x 15in tyres

DIMENSIONS:
Weight 2,140lb (972kg)

PERFORMANCE:
(Source: *Car South Africa*)
Max speed 95mph
0–60mph 15.6sec
30–50mph in top 9.8sec
50–70mph in top 12.9sec

US PRICE WHEN NEW: (AUGUST 1961)
PV544 Sport $2,195
PV544 Special
De Luxe $1,995

NUMBER MADE (TOTAL): 243,995
A (1958–1960) 99,495
B (1960–1961) 34,600
C (1961–1962) 37,900
D (1962–1963) 27,100
E (1963–1964) 24,200
F (1964–1965) 17,300
G (1965) 3,400

Notes:
The above figures relate to the PV544 Sport, although there was a standard car available with a 1,580cc engine developing 60bhp.

group. It had already been decided that the first cars would be shown in the autumn of the following year, so with such a tight deadline, there was no time to be wasted.

Despite there being little more than a year to complete the first running cars, there had been no decision made about the configuration that the new vehicle would have. A skilled engineer named Erik Jern was one of the senior members of the team, and he discussed with Petterson the possibilities open to them in terms of engine, transmission and body design. Having looked at some of the DKWs that were being produced at that time, the two decided that more and more car manufacturers would follow the front-wheel drive route taken by the German car maker.

So, having made a decision to explore the front-wheel drive option, a lot of time and effort was spent trying to construct a layout which would prove reliable in everyday use. Not only did it become clear that front-wheel drive would be inherently less reliable than a more conventional layout, but it also would have meant Volvo having to produce more components in-house than was desirable. At that time there simply were not enough companies around with the expertise or manufacturing capacity that Volvo would have needed, and so – towards the end of 1943 – a decision was made to use a

This 1944 prototype of the PV444 differed little from its standard production counterpart.

more conventional, rear-wheel drive configuration. To help things along, the design team for the new car bought a 1939 Hanomag two-door saloon to see how it was put together. The aim was to come up with designs for a car with unitary construction – something which Volvo had not done before, but of which Hanomag had experience.

While the exterior design was underway it became evident that the car's styling was heavily influenced by contemporary American designs – Petterson claimed Pontiac and Ford supplied most of the inspiration. After Gabrielsson and Larson had seen the scale clay models it was time for a full-size wooden mock-up to be built. Larson had reckoned that the original bonnet was too narrow, requesting that it be made wider.

Once he had given the go-ahead with the revised model it was crunch time – the decision had to be made on whether or not this was the design that was to allow the company to expand dramatically in the immediate post-war years. As was customary at that time, the wooden car was constructed and both Gabrielsson and Larson inspected it from every angle before concluding that this was the car that would sell in big numbers once the war was over. The exterior design was the only thing which had been signed off at that time however – there still remained the matter of engine, transmission, suspension and interior to be decided upon.

Reliability had to come before innovation, but when most of the engineers on the project suggested

a side-valve engine, Petterson and Jern were adamant that an overhead-valve unit should be used. Volvo had never used an overhead-valve engine in any of its cars before, but that did not mean the company's engineers felt them to be inherently unreliable. In the end it was decided that the powerplant would be a 1,414cc in-line four-cylinder unit, with overhead valves and three main bearings.

Although it would be nearly a year before the Second World War was over, Volvo decided that to promote the PV444 – which would become the first of its post-war models – it would

The Duett

Volvo's big innovations for 1953 were the van and estate car, which had been developed since the previous summer. Until then the PV445 was available as a chassis only, so that independent coachbuilders could add whatever rear bodywork they wanted, but by 1952 Volvo realised that by producing the PV445 the company was itself in a position to diversify. It also allowed customers to buy the cars they wanted, as the independent coachbuilders could not keep up with demand. Volvo dealers had been stocking independently built vehicles, but with supply being far short of demand it made sense for Volvo to bring production in-house to produce such cars more quickly. By doing this, the number of PV445s sold as a chassis only was necessarily much reduced, and before long production slowed to a trickle – although it was not until 1960 that the last one was built.

The in-house estate car was called the Duett, on account of its dual-purpose role of offering transport for both leisure and work, and it has become one of the most beloved

Volvos since the company started car production. This was a vehicle that combined commercial carrying capabilities with those of transporting a family around – a true dual-purpose car. Buyers could choose between a van with no side windows (the 445DS), a van with vestigial rear seat and small side windows (the 445DH), or an estate with a folding rear seat and full-length side windows, known as the 445PH.

The Duett was developed first and foremost as a light commercial vehicle, so not too much attention was paid to performance. Therefore, the 44bhp B4B engine did not give the car a great turn of speed, but as Swedish roads of the time were not particularly well built that didn't really matter. What did matter was reliability and practicality, and those were the things that the Duett could offer in spades.

As increasing numbers of people started buying the Duett in its estate car form the power was gradually increased, first to 51bhp (in 1955) and then to 60bhp. In the USA there was even a version available with the

70bhp B14A engine. Many of the Duett's developments mirrored those of the PV444 on which it was based, although they sometimes lagged behind by a year or two. So while the PV444 was superseded by the PV544 in 1958, the Duett did not receive the single-piece windscreen, four-speed gearbox or new dashboard until 1960. This model had been known as the PV445 Duett, but from the introduction of the new type of windscreen the car was now christened the P210 Duett. Two years later the B18 engine replaced the B16 unit (which had been introduced in 1958) and 12-volt electrics were fitted, but there was little in the way of development after this, and the car was taken out of production in 1969.

One of the best-loved and most practical Volvos ever, the Duett was full of character. This is an early example, recognisable by its split windscreen.

The PV444 was the first car built by Volvo that was truly mass-produced, with demand initially exceeding supply.

Throughout production the PV444's dashboard design did not change very much. This is one of the first cars.

Helmer Petterson

Helmer Petterson's background was in motorcycle racing and engineering, having started with Chicago-based Excelsior, one of the most innovative motorcycle makers of the time. Extrovert and outspoken, Petterson began working with Ford to manufacture gas-producer units in the wake of the outbreak of war, which had cut off fuel supplies.

Volvo began working on similar projects and Assar Gabrielsson consulted Petterson on the subject. Before long Petterson was being consulted on all sorts of things and it was only a matter of time before he became an official adviser to Volvo.

It was probably Petterson who was behind Volvo's acquisition of a Hanomag – a car which was analysed very closely during the design of Volvo's PV444. He reckoned that in the wake of the war, fuel taxes would be increased and motoring would become much less affordable. Economy cars would be the only way of turning in a profit he said, and sure enough, this proved to be the case.

The PV series which resulted from this project was a massive success and Petterson was also involved in coming up with a successor to it.

His PV454 was too similar to the earlier PV series however and in the end it was Jan Wilsgaard's Amazon design which went into production.

put on an exhibition of its products. Everything the company produced was displayed, and between 1 and 10 September 1944, no fewer than 148,437 people flocked to see the wares of Volvo at Stockholm's Royal Tennis Hall. Each day there was the chance to win a PV444 and people who signed up to buy the new model would be able to purchase it at just SKr4,800 – the same price as had been asked for the very first Volvo in 1927.

In the event, 2,300 people signed up to take delivery of the PV444, but the first examples were not delivered to their owners until 1947 – by which time the price had risen to SKr6,050. Those who had signed up early were able to buy the cars at the reduced price or sell their place in the queue to people who had not been quite so far-sighted. A shortage of raw materials had led to the delay in getting series production underway, but once supplies started to come on

stream it allowed Volvo to expand rapidly, with the car being very much in demand.

On a global scale there was nothing especially revolutionary about the PV444, but for Volvo it marked several firsts, notably a semi-monocoque construction and an overhead-valve engine. The four-cylinder engine drove the rear wheels through a conventional three-speed manual gearbox with synchromesh on second and top gears. The car's name is reputed to stem from the fact that it offered four cylinders, seating for four and 40 horsepower – or maybe just the fact that its design was settled upon in 1944! Compared with the UK and America, the car was innovative, with its coil-sprung suspension, but compared with French and German designs it was less advanced.

In February 1945, the Swedish General Strike caused havoc with Volvo's plans to continue to develop

the PV444 before it went on sale. Luckily, a prototype and a pair of test cars had already been built and fuel rationing was overcome with special dispensation obtained from the government. By the summer of that year the prototype had covered 30,000km (18,750 miles) visiting all 76 dealerships around the country, allowing everybody to take a look at the new car – and it proved a great hit.

A few teething troubles with the B4B engines used in the test cars were ironed out and by 1946 the PV444 had become a paragon of reliability. But with the war not such a distant memory it was not going to prove easy putting the car into production as there was a severe shortage of raw materials. Gabrielsson's aim was to sign contracts with American suppliers to sell the necessary steel to Volvo, but they were not interested – the US car industry was desperate for the

Despite the exterior colours of the PV series often being very conservative, the interior colours could be somewhat lurid!

The rear suspension was changed to semi-elliptic leaf springs and double-acting hydraulic dampers, all of which was attached directly to the chassis to make bespoke bodywork much easier to fit.

Known as the PV445, this development allowed new variants to be developed very quickly, easily and cheaply – the first of which were light commercial vehicles capable of carrying around half a ton. The first of these was shown by Volvo in 1949, but it was not long before ambulances, hearses and even convertibles were being built by independent coachbuilders. One of the most popular conversions was an estate, built by Gripkarosser, and this was the catalyst that prompted Volvo to develop its own estate car, which would be introduced in 1953.

In September 1950, the PV444B was announced, offering small improvements over the original model. Focusing on minor interior modifications and significant changes to the bumper design, there was also a development that was seen as anything but an improvement. It was the adoption of a T-shaped bar on the roof to house the indicators. Called the Fixlight by Volvo, everybody else called it less complimentary things, the favourite term being the cuckoo on the roof.

Several decades before high-level brake lights became the norm, Gabrielsson reckoned roof-mounted indicators were the way forward. Leaks through the mounting holes and the inability to fit a roof rack were problems he hadn't foreseen however and by the summer of 1952 the turn signals were mounted conventionally in the door pillars – which was just as well because the Fixlight was outlawed from January 1953.

material and there just wasn't enough to go round.

The answer was found by sending a prototype to America so the steel suppliers had something to see. That seemed to do the trick, as a contract was signed shortly afterwards and it looked as though production could finally begin in 1947. By March of that year the order book had to be closed such was the demand for the car, and a turning point was reached in 1949: this was the first year that Volvo built more cars than trucks and buses. Until that point, car manufacturing was almost an offshoot of the bus and truck operation.

With production fully underway the PV444 was gradually improved, attention being paid to refinement and reliability as much as possible. All the hard work had certainly paid off as in one of its first post-war tests *The Motor* commented that the PV444 was sprightly enough, remarkably economical and very comfortable to ride in – as well as

rewarding to drive.

Until the end of 1949, the PV444 had been available only in black and with just one interior colour scheme – yellow and green. Offering an alternative was the PV444S, 700 of which were produced with light blue paint, grey and red interior trim and a plethora of chrome embellishments. However, unless you already had a PV444 on order and could afford to pay the extra to trade up, the special model was 'out of bounds'.

After the PV444 had been introduced, Volvo realised that the car's monocoque construction meant the producing of one-off bodies for special customers was very difficult, if not impossible. Developing other variants was also not as easy as it had been previously, so the rather unusual step was taken of moving backwards by introducing a PV444 with a separate chassis. To be fair, it was not really a complete PV444 but the engine, electrics, transmission, brakes and front suspension which were carried over to a new model.

Series identification

When the first PV444s were sold in 1947 they did not have any other series identification, but when a slightly 'tweaked' model was launched in September 1950 it was known as the PV444B, making its predecessor known retrospectively as the PV444A, or the 'A' model – while the Special was retrospectively known as the AS. The main change was the adoption of the Fixlight indicators (see main text).

In June 1951, the PV444C and 'CS' superseded the 'B' model, but changes were slight. A 1½in wider track and 15in wheels replaced the previously fitted 16in items, but at that stage supply was still well short of demand so it made little difference to buyers, who snapped up whatever cars were available.

The PV444D and 'DS' were introduced in August 1952, but despite the car being badged as a development of the series, amendments were no more far-reaching than in the previous change of tag as they were limited to a new type of optional heater, and the demise of the Fixlight, replaced by side-mounted flashing indicators.

April 1953 saw the launch of the 'E' and 'ES' cars which lasted until December 1954. Once again, there were no major changes, the most significant development being the introduction of a heater as standard, although a price reduction in 1953 was a welcome if somewhat unusual move.

The next versions of the PV444 were the 'H' and 'HS' derivatives ('F' and 'G' were skipped) and it was the first time that the changes were significant. Narrower pillars and larger front and rear screens made the cabin lighter.

The next model, the PV444K, appeared in December 1955. A more powerful, 51bhp, engine was introduced this time although the grille design was also changed to make it look more up to date.

When the final version of the PV444 was introduced in January 1957 – the 'L' and 'LS' models – there was another jump in power, but this time it was through the fitment of the larger B16 engine. The same as the unit fitted to the Amazon, the 1.6-litre engine generated 60bhp and attention had also been paid to refinement levels, better soundproofing and insulation. Seat-belt mountings were also fitted as standard and the vacuum-operated windscreen wipers were replaced by an electric system.

The PV544A arrived in August 1958 and a year later the B series superseded it, with better gearboxes, a higher-quality interior and a wider range of colours. The PV544C of August 1961 brought with it the B18 engine and adjustments to the front suspension, the adoption of a 12-volt electrical system and better interior and exterior trim.

For the 1963 model-year D series there was better rustproofing and a wider choice of colours, while the 1964 model year cars, first shown in August 1963, had a new roof-lining, green panel lighting and were known as E series cars.

The PV544F was announced in August 1964 with smaller hubcaps, different wheels and emblems on the boot lid; production would be halted just a few months later, but there was a PV544G shown in August 1965. The greatest change for this derivative was that the Sport version had a 95bhp engine in place of the 90bhp unit fitted previously.

Although there were few radical changes throughout the life of the PV series, there was a gradual evolution.

The PV warranty

The cat was well and truly put among the pigeons in 1954 when Volvo announced that it was offering a five-year warranty on the PV444 as part of the purchase cost. That in itself was not that big a deal, as it wasn't a guarantee as such, but was actually a comprehensive insurance cover given away free with each car bought.

The car's owner still had to buy third-party insurance cover, but Volvo would pay for the cost of any repairs exceeding SKr200 in the event of any accident – regardless of whose fault it was.

Sweden's insurance industry took exception to such an offer and accused the company of unfair practices. The initial idea had been Assar Gabrielsson's in 1954, so it was he who ended up in the dock in 1956 when Volvo was taken to court over the warranty. But it wasn't until September 1958 that the matter was finally resolved when the case was dismissed by Sweden's Supreme Court.

In that time Volvo had made great capital of the benefits offered to owners, with plenty of case histories being featured in advertisements of cars written off and replaced for SKr200. As the warranty was valid for only five years, Volvo had set up its own insurance company (named Volvia) to allow owners to buy an insurance policy from their vehicle's maker. It was not until shortly after Ford's acquisition of Volvo in 1999 that this insurance scheme was wound up.

Throughout the PV444's lifetime, Volvo could easily sell every car it made. All these PV444s would have been sold before they were built.

By January 1952, a mere 25,000 PV444s had been produced. A factory-fitted heater was available from autumn 1952, so buyers did not have to go to an outside manufacturer to have a heater supplied, and changes to the steering and electrical systems were incorporated. But aside from that, it was business as usual, with prices now pegged at SKr10,860 for the Standard car and SKr11,415 for the Special.

A major milestone for Volvo was reached in 1955, as it was the year in which the first car from the company was exported to America – the start of a huge success story for the car maker. The first Volvo sent to America had been the prototype PV444 in 1947, but as Assar Gabrielsson neared retirement in 1955, a concerted effort to export cars to the USA started to gather momentum. The first dealership was set up in Fort Worth, Texas, by Nils Sefeldt, who was an aeronautical engineer with a passion for cars. He borrowed heavily and

Horsepower rating

Trying to understand different types of horsepower ratings is never easy, as there are usually so many, but with Volvos there are really only two to contend with – the DIN figure and the SAE. The DIN horsepower rating is achieved by running an engine with all its ancillaries fitted, whereas the SAE rating is obtained by running the powerplant with all of these removed. The difference normally equates to around 10 per cent, so taking the B16B engine with twin carburettors as an example, using the DIN rating there is 76bhp on offer, but move over to the SAE rating and there is 85bhp on tap – a significant improvement.

travelled to New York to collect the first car, driving it back to Texas. His first five cars arrived soon after, but they proved difficult to sell. He did manage to shift them eventually, but the next five proved just as difficult. On the verge of giving up, things started to pick up in Spring 1956, and from then on, the sales network expanded with the USA quickly becoming Volvo's biggest market.

With precise controls, reasonable acceleration and a comfortable ride, a PV – this is a PV544 – is a very practical classic. The red badge on the grille indicates that this is a later model, fitted with a 1.8-litre engine.

The PV544's dash is quite different from its predecessor's, but still very simple.

Volvo had already exported cars to other countries as far back as the 1930s, and to give trans-Atlantic sales a boost, the PV444 Export was introduced, based on the H series PV444. Introduced at the 1955 California Auto Show, it wasn't built especially for the US market as examples would also be sold in Denmark, Belgium, Norway and South America. Whereas for most other manufacturers an export model meant something with more equipment, for Volvo it meant the opposite as the cars featured a lower specification to make them easier for US dealers to sell, thanks to their

lower price. On these models. aluminium paint replaced the chrome trim of the exterior brightwork, the amount of which was reduced to a minimum. The interior trim was also reduced to the bare minimum, with very basic seating and the heater was removed. A fifth of the 444s built during 1955 were Export models, some of which were sold in the home market, but without a heater it wasn't easy to sell such cars in Sweden – car buyers had come to expect *some* comfort in the harsh Swedish winters!

In the spring of 1956 the PV444 was first shown on the East coast of America, at the New York Auto Show. As well as the reduced trim levels, there were other modifications made for US-market cars. Tubular nudge bars, called

'American rails', were fitted to the front and rear bumpers and the indicators were moved from the door pillars to the leading edges of the front wings. To demonstrate how important the American market was to Volvo, a special edition PV444 was created especially for that market. Called the PV444 California, the car had either white or yellow paintwork with black interior trim. The car was a hit and within a year Volvo's popularity was second only to Volkswagen (in terms of imported cars) in the Western states, and 100 dealers had been appointed. The reasons for the PV444's success were manifold, but the most frequently quoted were the reliability and high quality of finish although the car's competition success also enticed some to part with their cash.

The drophead PV445

With the availability of a chassis-only PV444 (named the PV445) for special-bodied vehicles, the floodgates were opened for coach-builders to create their own interpretations of a convertible Volvo. Nevertheless, there was hardly a flood of cars built: between three different coachbuilders, fewer than 40 examples were ever made.

Valbo and Ringborg built around 22 and 15 cars respectively, with very similar designs while Stockholm-based Nordberg – which had built special-bodied six-cylinder Volvos before the war – also constructed a drophead that was a bit more flamboyant.

The PV445 chassis was available from 1949 until 1960, when it was replaced by the PV544-based P2101 chassis. This continued to be available until 1962, but by the middle of the 1950s nobody was building drophead Volvos any more. Although most of the cars created still survive, there are not many left that are still usable.

Few drophead examples of the PV series were built. This example by Valbo is one of just 22 made.

The first PV544s featured a 1.6-litre engine but from 1961 there was the option of a 1.8-litre unit.

In January 1957, the 1.4-litre engine was replaced by the 1,582cc B16A unit, which was exactly the same engine as used in the new Amazon. Developing 60bhp at 4,500rpm, the powerplant was far more torquey than its predecessor. At the same time as the new engine was introduced the vacuum-operated windscreen wipers were replaced by an electric system and there were some significant changes to the exterior design, in preparation for the car's replacement the following year. There was a new, mesh radiator grille in place of the bars found on previous cars and the chrome waist trim was positioned lower down. New rear lamps were also fitted, which

soon became known as 'maiden's tits' on account of their rounded shape and smaller size.

Even in 1957, after the PV444 had been around for nearly a decade, Volvo still had a few tricks up its sleeve. A four-speed gearbox replaced the three-speed unit, which had been fitted since production of the car had started. A long-overdue development, this allowed the newer engine's torque characteristics to be better utilised, but it was reserved for export cars only – the Amazon was the only Volvo that Swedish buyers could buy with the four-speed unit. With 10,000 cars going to the USA in 1957 and the cars' popularity increasing all the time, it was clear that Volvo simply did not have enough production capacity to build all the PV444s and Amazons that buyers wanted – and the introduction of the PV544 didn't do anything to dampen demand.

The PV544 superseded the PV444

in 1958. Using virtually the same bodyshell as its predecessor, the new car had a larger engine and room for five people instead of just four – hence the 544 tag. The extra space was created by the use of a rear seat more than 6in (150mm) wider and thinner front seats to allow more legroom. Although few people expected Volvo to continue producing a car which had already been around for nearly a decade, it all made sense – especially as the car was still incredibly popular. Not only was the body tooling long since paid for, but with a bit of a tweak here and there the car could see service for another decade before finally being put out to pasture. And besides, it allowed Volvo to have a two-car product range rather than just the one.

Volvo spent just three million kronor on its 'new' car by updating the old design, whereas an all-new model would have cost the company at least 35 million kronor. The car's

The Philip prototype

When the PV444 was first shown in 1944, the American influence in its styling was immediately obvious. So when a replacement model was proposed in the early 1950s, it was probably no surprise that the finished prototype would not have looked out of place on the streets of Detroit with its rear wheel spats, heavy chrome bumpers and whitewall tyres. The car was the Philip, so-called because its specification was settled on Sweden's Filip day (2 May) in 1950.

Designed by Jan Wilsgaard, the Philip was a proposal to take Volvo upmarket from the PV444, the company's only offering in the post-war years. With styling heavily influenced by the contemporary Kaiser, the natural powerplant for such a car was a V8 engine, mated to an automatic gearbox. As Volvo did not produce such an item a unit had to be produced from scratch. In the event, the Philip did not go into production with only one example built, but a modified version of the V8 developed specially for it did go on to power Volvo trucks.

The V8 engineered by the company had a displacement of 3,559cc with both block and heads being of cast iron. With wedge-type combustion chambers, overhead valves and a compression ratio of 6.8:1, the unit developed 120bhp. In a car weighing nearly 31¼cwt (1,587kg) that did not allow for very impressive performance, but at least 100mph was just about possible.

By the time the car had been developed sufficiently to make it reliable Volvo had changed its mind about going too far upmarket. It had taken two years to build the car and in that time things had changed both in the automotive world and within Volvo. The project was canned but the car survives in Volvo's Gothenburg museum.

The V8 Volvo that never was – the Philip was more like an American car than something originating in Sweden.

durability was also well proven and through continuous development of the model, the PV was still competitive from a performance and driving point of view. Indeed, in America, the country where the car was at its most popular, the PV was nicer to drive than most of its home-grown rivals. And to cap it all, whereas the typical American car depreciated by 40 per cent in its first year, the Volvo lost just eight per cent of its value in the same period – it was no wonder Volvo was reluctant to replace the car with an all-new model.

By sticking with a well-established car Volvo could focus on addressing the shortcomings of the existing model, so the cramped interior and poor visibility were the key areas to be tackled. As a result, the most significant change externally was a larger, one-piece curved windscreen – all PV444s had featured a split windscreen with flat glass. The rear window was also larger and the tail lights changed in appearance. Although changes on the outside were slight, there were more significant ones under the skin. The steering box was now more responsive and passenger space was increased significantly. Rear seatbelt mountings were now standard as was a padded safety dash.

In 1969, four years after the PV544 had gone out of production, Volvo's decision to stick with the basic formula of the PV444 would be vindicated, when 11 Volvo dealers smashed up a 1958 example of the PV544 in New York. They were pro-testing publicly that Volvos were made too well – something that was at odds with their need to make a profit. Owners didn't need to replace their cars as frequently and warranties were rarely called upon because the cars were so reliable. Having turned it over and smashed it up, the car was pretty much wrecked. But one of the dealers decided to see if it would still start, and of course as soon as he turned the key the engine burst into life. Proof, if any were needed, that Volvos were streets

ahead of their competitors when it came to durability . . .

By the time the PV544 had superseded the PV444, Volvo had started to raise its profile in a big way through its cars' success in motorsport. The rate at which Volvos were notching up victories in the hands of such legendary drivers as Tom Trana and Gunnar Andersson did not do the cars' sales any harm at all. As well as the positive publicity generated by this competition success, sales of the PV444 had been increased significantly by offering buyers more choice. So Volvo reckoned that if the range was increased even further, yet more people would opt for one of its cars. The plan worked, after no fewer than four different versions of the PV544 had been introduced. The PV544 Standard was the no-frills choice, with a 60bhp B16A engine, three-speed gearbox and no choice of colour other than black. Priced at SKr9,250, the Standard cost SKr270 less than the Special I, which featured higher equipment levels and plusher interior trim. If this still wasn't highly specified enough there was always the Special II at SKr10,750, complete with four-speed gearbox and more colour choices. But for those who could afford SKr10,375 there was the top model, the PV544 Sport. This was fitted with the 85bhp B16B engine that until now had been reserved for cars sold in America only, and to make the price more palatable there were a few extra bits of equipment fitted such as front seatbelts, a trip recorder and headlight flashers.

The success of the PV series was partly accounted for by the fact that Volvo had gone to great trouble to tailor the car for each export market. As a result, there were over 100 different versions of the car available around the world, although they only varied in detail. It wasn't until 1960 that any significant changes were made to the PV544, when the PV544B appeared. This had an all-synchromesh three-speed gearbox or the option of a four-speed unit and

the interior design was slightly more luxurious. The bigger changes however, were reserved for the following year, when the PV544C was introduced, complete with the five-bearing B18 engine first seen in the P1800. In single-carburettor form a healthy 75bhp was on tap, but if the B18D engine was chosen, the twin SU carburettors gave an even healthier 90bhp. This endowed the car with genuine 100mph (160kph) performance – a far cry from the 70–75mph (113–121kph) maximum of the PV444 of just five years earlier. At the same time as the B18 engine becoming available, the electrical system was upgraded to a 12-volt layout and changes were made to the interior, exterior trim, front suspension and steering.

Although the numerous trim levels had proved to be successful, they were also confusing to many buyers and because of this, the range was rationalised slightly, with the Standard and Special I being combined to make the Favorit, complete with 75bhp engine and three-speed gearbox. Buyers with a bit more money to spend could opt for the Special, with an extra gear ratio, more brightwork and whitewall tyres as well as opening rear windows and a wider choice of colours. The range-topper was still the Sport, which now had a 90bhp version of the B18 engine, but after the C-model had been launched, development of the PV544 was half-hearted. Volvo chose to let sales of the car just tick over, resources being devoted instead to the 1800 and to development of the future 140 model.

The PV544 was at its peak in 1959, when no fewer than 51,560 cars were delivered. From then on it was a gradual decline and on 20 October 1965, nearly a decade after the introduction of the Amazon, the last PV544 was built. Considering the Amazon had been introduced in 1956 to supersede the PV range, it is a testament to the PV544's popularity that it lived so long.

The Elizabeth I and II protypes

In 1952, a Swedish entrepreneur named Gosta Wennberg was considering the possibility of producing PV444s with exclusive bodywork. To see how viable the project would be he commissioned Vignale to produce a two-door, four-seater car on a PV444 Duett chassis. The car was completed in 1953, and there were strong overtones of contemporary Alfa Romeo in its design.

When the car was despatched to Volvo for them to see, there were nods of approval all round. The styling was certainly elegant but the interior packaging was cramped considering the car's external dimensions. So when Volvo commissioned Vignale to produce a successor to the original prototype,

the floorpan from a standard PV444 was supplied.

Before Vignale even started building the second prototype the Swedish press had come up with a name for the first car – which Wennberg had been parading around to get as much publicity as he could. The press had started calling it the Elizabeth, to connect it to the Philip prototype seen the previous year – this being in the wake of the coronation of Queen Elizabeth II that year. As a result, the second prototype was instantly known as the Elizabeth II, as it closely followed the design of the first car.

The second car, completed in 1954, was even more graceful than the first, but it still did not fit in with Volvo's project plans and it all came to

nothing. Wennberg soon realised that building 200 cars at SKr20,000 wasn't viable and everything ground to a halt. The significance of Wennberg's car should not be underestimated however, because Jan Wilsgaard's '55' of 1953 (see Chapter 3) took many of its styling details from it, and that car heavily influenced the Amazon.

The Elizabeth project started out as a study in producing bespoke bodywork for the PV444, but the sums just didn't add up.

Replacing the PV444

By the early 1950s the PV444 was beginning to look dated because many of its competitors were starting to boast full-width styling. A completely new car was not going to be possible because of budgetary constraints but Helmer Petterson reckoned that did not mean something pretty radical was out of the question.

Petterson had been asked by Assar Gabrielsson to come up with something to replace the PV series and the result was the PV454, which used the floorpan and running gear of the PV444, but which featured a completely new body. This was heavily inspired by the Raymond Loewy-designed Studebakers of the period, with flowing rear wings which were still separate from the body and a divided-nostril front grille. There was still a split windscreen but the rear window was greatly enlarged, and when Gabrielsson saw the car he approved it immediately.

In the meantime, Gustaf Larson had been working on a different PV444 replacement with Jan Wilsgaard. Unusually, Gabrielsson and Larson had not communicated with each other and although the signal had been given to take the PV454 into production, when the conflict became apparent soon after, it was the Larson/Wilsgaard project, known internally as '55' which was preferred, although this would be changed substantially before reaching the showrooms.

Another potential PV444 replacement was the PV179, development of which had started in 1952, five years after the PV444 had gone on sale with introduction planned for 1954, ten years after the PV444 had first been shown. Another of Jan Wilsgaard's designs, the PV179 was based on the PV444's chassis, which meant the same wheelbase, engine, gearbox and axle had to be used.

The suspension was not carried over in its entirety however as some bespoke parts were manufactured for this prototype – although in the event, they were nearly identical to those fitted to the Amazon when it was introduced in 1956.

Although the mechanicals were largely familiar, the sheet metal certainly wasn't, as it was all new, but Wilsgaard had to retain the PV444's roofline. This meant it was difficult to produce a design which looked good from all angles, and the resulting two-door fastback with vestigial fins and narrow grille with recessed headlamps on either side did look slightly clumsy from some viewpoints, although overall it was not displeasing.

But despite the fact that most of the managers within Volvo liked the car very much, Helmer Petterson most certainly didn't. His services had been retained by Volvo as a consultant on design issues and he reckoned the car was too big for the PV444 mechanicals that were planned for it. As a result the project was cancelled and it was then that the Margaret Rose name was conjured up. Pictures of the aborted project were released to the Swedish press and they came up with the Margaret Rose name to maintain the British Royal family theme which had been started with the Philip and which continued with the Elizabeth cars.

Only one PV179 prototype was built, and it has not survived as Raymond Eknor, a Volvo engineer, rolled it and destroyed it in the process.

This, the PV179, was the car that could have replaced the PV444, but in the end, a revised design was introduced instead – the PV544.

Volvo in motorsport

In 1955, with the Saab factory team racking up wins in just about every major rally on the calendar, it would have made perfect sense for Volvo to enter some of its cars into world-class rallying. It was decided though that competition was unnecessary as buyers were already well aware of the strength of the company's cars. In 1956, Gunnar Engellau stated publicly that rallying cars was 'as much use as dog racing' but as early as 1949 a PV444 had been entered privately in that year's Monte Carlo Rally by Hilding Ohlsson, Martin Carstedt and Stig Cederholm. Although they made no great impression, the following year the same team finished 12th overall – a good result for a bunch of privateers.

The turning point came in 1957 when a PV444 was entered privately in the Rally to the Midnight Sun, which was Sweden's qualifying event for the European Rally Championship. In the same year the Norwegian Rally was won by another pair of privateers in

their PV444, but this was only the start, as the following year Gunnar Andersson burst on to the scene and secured a placing in just about every race he entered. Andersson had started rallying a Jaguar XK120 in 1953 and in 1957 he bought his first Volvo, a PV444. Junking the factory-fitted engine in favour of an American-spec 75bhp unit, Andersson planned to compete in the Acropolis, Midnight Sun, German and Tulip rallies in 1958 – all with his own money.

On his first outing, in the Acropolis Rally, Andersson achieved a third place – and his competitors were immediately suspicious of what was nestling under his car's bonnet. He ended up having to strip the engine and have it compared with a showroom-fresh standard car, but he was guilty of nothing underhand so he retained his trophies and managed to become Volvo's first works driver into the bargain. Gunner Engellau rang him up to ask him if he would be interested in driving factory-prepared rally cars and continue his success in the company's name instead of his own, to which he agreed.

By 1963, Volvo was shouting very loudly about its motorsport successes, using images of what looked like more or less standard Amazons being campaigned in rallies. Tom Trana, Sylvia Osterberg and Gunnar Andersson were all notching up one victory after another during the 1963 and 1964 rallying seasons in both Amazons and PV544s. By this stage Volvo was running adverts which did not even talk about road cars – merely its cars' successes in rallying, track racing and even economy runs throughout the world.

There were even short biographies of the works drivers included in these advertisements. The company had finally realised that by entering cars which, to the outside world, were essentially the same as those found in its showrooms, buyers would very quickly latch onto the fact that the cars they would be buying from the Swedish company would be equally durable in everyday use.

It was the PV444 which launched Volvo's motorsport presence. The most successful drivers were Gunnar Andersson and Tom Trana.

Driving

With anywhere between 40bhp and 85bhp on tap, the performance of a PV can vary wildly between lethargic and sprightly. Get behind the wheel of one of the last PV544s and you will find the car a joy to drive with anything up to 95bhp for the last of the Sport models while an early PV444 with just 40bhp under your right foot can be painfully slow when it gets hilly.

Somewhere between these two extremes lies the more typical PV – the 51bhp, 60bhp or 70bhp cars which are pleasant to drive and surprisingly usable in modern traffic. With decent acceleration and good refinement, the mid-range (in terms of power) PV444 and PV544 make a great alternative to more predictable classics.

Perhaps the performance on offer is the least important of the various aspects of driving one of these Volvos as it is the feel of the controls

Outwardly there was little to distinguish the PV544 from the PV444, the single-piece windscreen being the most obvious difference.

that makes the cars so endearing. The brakes are good although they could have a bit more bite, and the steering is surprisingly free of play and more direct than you might expect. Even the gearchange refuses to be vague, despite its long lever and it has a precise action mated to a well-weighted clutch. Not only that, but the ride is compliant and with radial tyres there is plenty of grip when you come to a corner and you find that you are travelling faster than you thought.

The PV series evolved steadily over nearly two decades, with attention paid to ergonomics, but you will not find the seats very comfortable in any of the cars for long journeys. Although the seats could be better, at least there's no shortage of space for four people to travel in comfort – and in the case of the PV544, there is ample room for five.

Tuning and modifying

If you're going to tune a PV it is unlikely that you will be starting with a B14-engined car. But if you

do, the first thing that you will need to do is swap the 1.4-litre engine for a B16 unit. Once you have done that you can start doing some worthwhile tuning modifications. It is then a case of performing the classic tuning modifications of porting the cylinder head, uprating the camshaft and improving the fuelling. Fitting twin SU carburettors to take the engine up to Sport specification is worthwhile, but don't overdo it – 1¾in carbs is as far as you can go without suffering overfuelling problems. Fitting a four-branch manifold will also bring useful power gains, but you will have to have one fabricated specially as there is nothing available from any other Volvo model which will bolt on.

If you have a B16 engine it is not very easy to upgrade to a B18 unit because it's a completely different engine which is built around a 12-volt electrical system instead of the earlier cars' six-volt system. The swap can be made, but it is expensive because so many electrical components have to be changed in the process, along with the gearbox, brakes and clutch. On this

basis you are better off tuning the B16 engine or buying a B18-engined car, but one change that is worth making is the fitment of a B18 clutch, which means making minor changes to the flywheel. This will allow you to ditch the spring-operated unit for a diaphragm one, the latter type being much easier to get parts for.

If you have a B18-equipped PV you can either tune the 1.8-litre engine or go for the ultimate car by opting for a B20 powerplant. A tuned B20 engine in a PV would be a bit crazy, so we'll assume that a tuned B18 engine or a standard B20 is as far as you are likely to go in this car. If you do decide to go for all-out power and you want to uprate the larger engine, it is essentially a case of performing the classic tuning modifications which means porting, polishing, a spicier camshaft and larger carburettors.

If you are sticking with the B18 engine it is much the same as if you were going to tune the B20 unit – it's the same upgrades but if you're going to fit bigger carburettors it's not worth fitting anything larger than a pair of SU HS6s or the engine will have too much fuel. It is possible to fit Webers but the car will drink petrol and there are clearance problems in the engine bay because the clutch master cylinder and steering column will be in the way.

Tuning a B18-engined PV without fitting the two-branch manifold from a post-1966 Volvo is pointless as the standard-fit single-branch unit restricts the engine's ability to breathe. It is possible to buy a 2in free-flow system off the shelf and this, when combined with the two-branch manifold, makes a significant difference to the power output.

Whichever engine you have fitted and whatever stage it is tuned to, upgrading the brakes to Amazon discs is a good idea – and for some of the wilder upgrades it is essential. While you're at it, the rear drums should also be swapped for Amazon units because they are easier to maintain. You're unlikely to need a servo and because PV suspension used telescopic shock absorbers from the outset, it is easy to fit more durable Konis or Bilsteins without having to make any modifications.

Buying

1. You will search in vain for a right-hand drive PV as the car was not officially imported into the UK, so only left-hand drive cars were produced. However, finding a PV444 or PV544 at all in the UK won't prove very easy as very few cars made it to these shores.

2. The chassis legs are prone to rot, where the subframe bolts on and if not caught in time the engine can end up falling out as its mounts will fail.

3. Other rot spots include the boot floor, the outriggers and the leading edges of the tops of the rear wings, where they are located by captive nuts.

4. The suspension is pre-war and American in its design, and as a result you can expect the upper and lower trunnions to be worn along with the kingpins. It is also a common occurrence to find fracturing of the wishbones near to where they are mounted to the sub-frame.

5. The brakes work fine if they are set up properly, but they require more maintenance than a conventional disc/drum system. Some owners prefer to use the front disc set-up from the Amazon, which bolts straight on – fit a servo as well and you will enjoy much-improved efficiency and feel.

6. Engine parts are very hard to come by, those for the 1.4-litre version being especially difficult to source. To help the bearings as much as possible it is essential that a proper Volvo oil filter is used, this being fitted with a non-return valve. Anything less will starve the bearings of oil on start up, so listen to the engine from a cold start up to make sure the bearings aren't on their way out.

7. Clutches aren't very robust, wearing down to the metal alarmingly quickly in some cases. For this reason it is worth modifying the flywheel so that the later (diaphragm) type of clutch can be fitted instead. Check for vibration in the driveline, caused by wear in the propshaft couplings.

8. The gearboxes are simple and tough, but you should listen to hear if top gear is quieter than the other ratios. If it is, you're going to have to shell out for a new gearbox before too long.

9. Cars that have been used for long-distance journeys or a lot of high-speed travel will probably be the worse for wear. Low gearing means the engine will have to work hard and once it's worn there will be a noticeable knock from the cylinder head – signalling it is time for a replacement to be fitted.

10. As 1.4-litre and 1.6-litre cars are fitted with six-volt electrics, parts for which are very hard to find, you are better off looking for a 1.8-litre car which is not only fitted with 12-volt electrics but is also much more usable.

The Amazon *series*

Perhaps one of the most contrived press shots ever, but amusing with it. Volvo had taken quite a hold on the domestic market by the time the Amazon arrived, although Volvo fever is perhaps an overstatement!

By the early 1950s, Volvo had to start thinking about a replacement for the PV series, knowing that it would take several years to design and engineer something that would maintain the Volvo reputation of longevity and dependability. Jan Wilsgaard was charged with coming up with a car which could supersede the PV444 and which would compete with the Opel Kapitan and some of the smaller Mercedes cars.

Wilsgaard initially came up with a pair of designs, one of which was an evolution of the PV444 while the other was something quite different – a new, larger car. It was decided to go with the all-new design, the rationale being that it could be sold alongside the PV series for several years, giving Volvo a two-model range in the process. Considering it was launched as a more upmarket Volvo than the PV444, rather than the replacement it was originally

121 with B16A engine
1957–1961

ENGINE:
Four cylinders in line, iron block and head
Bore x stroke	79.4mm x 80mm
Capacity	1,583cc
Valvegear	Overhead valve
Compression ratio	7.4:1
Fuelling	Single Zenith carburettor
Maximum power	66bhp (SAE) at 4,500rpm
Maximum torque	85lb ft at 2,500rpm

TRANSMISSION:
Rear-wheel drive
Three-speed synchro on second and third
Final drive ratio   4.56:1

SUSPENSION:
Front: Independent with coil springs, telescopic dampers, wishbones, anti-roll bar
Rear: Live axle, coil springs, telescopic dampers, Panhard rod, torque arms

STEERING:
Cam and roller   3.5 turns lock-to-lock

BRAKES:
Front & Rear: Drum
Servo assistance standard from November 1958

WHEELS/TYRES:
Steel disc wheels with 5.90 x 15in tubeless whitewall tyres

BODYWORK:
Four-door saloon of unitary construction

DIMENSIONS:
Length	14ft 7in (4.45m)
Wheelbase	8ft 6in (2.60m)
Track	4ft 4in (1.32m)
Width	5ft 4in (1.62m)
Height	4ft 11in (1.51m)

WEIGHT: 2,400lb (1,090kg)

PERFORMANCE: (Source: *The Autocar*)
Max speed	94mph
0–60mph	14sec
30–50mph in top	9.7sec
50–70mph in top	12.5sec

PRICE WHEN NEW (JUNE 1958):
Four-door saloon: SKr12,600 (£868, but not officially imported into the UK)

NUMBER MADE:
Four-door	234,209
Two-door	359,917
Estate (Duett)	73,196

NOTES:
Overdrive was optional from 1960, as was an all-synchro gearbox. A four-speed all-synchro gearbox was optional from 1958 and for the 1961 model year an automatic transmission was available.

122S with B16B engine March
1958–1961

As 121 except:
ENGINE:
Compression ratio	8.2:1
Fuelling	Twin SU carburettors
Maximum power	85bhp (SAE) at 5,500rpm
Maximum torque	87lb ft at 3,000rpm

TRANSMISSION: Four-speed all-synchro

WEIGHT: 2,315lb (1,050kg)

PERFORMANCE: (Source: *The Motor*)
Max speed:	93mph
0–60mph	17.8sec
30–50mph in top	12.4sec
50–70mph in top	18.3sec

UK PRICE WHEN NEW (January 1959):
Four-door saloon   £1,399

121, 131, 221 with B18A engine
1961–1968

ENGINE:
Four cylinders in line, iron block and iron head
Bore x stroke	84mm x 80mm
Capacity	1,778cc
Valvegear	Overhead-valve
Compression ratio	8.5:1
Fuelling	Single Zenith carburettor
Maximum power	75bhp (net) at 4,500rpm (85bhp from August 1966)
Maximum torque	101lb ft at 2,800rpm

TRANSMISSION:
Rear-wheel-drive
Four-speed all-synchro
Saloon final drive ratio   4.1:1
Estate final drive ratio   4.56:1

SUSPENSION:
Front: Independent with coil springs, telescopic dampers, wishbones, anti-roll bar
Rear: Live axle, coil springs, telescopic dampers, Panhard rod

STEERING:
Cam and roller   Turns lock-to-lock   3.25

BRAKES:
Front: Disc   Rear: Drum
No servo assistance available

WHEELS/TYRES:
Pressed steel wheels with 5.90 x 15in tyres

WEIGHT:
Two-door saloon	2,357lb (1,070kg)
Four-door saloon	2,400lb (1,090kg)
Estate	2,621lb (1,190kg)

PERFORMANCE: (Source: *The Autocar*)
Max speed	90mph
0–60mph	17.6sec
30–50mph in top	10.1sec
50–70mph in top	14.7sec

UK PRICE WHEN NEW (April 1965):
Four-door saloon   £1,022

123GT with B18 engine
1966–1970

As 121 with B18 engine except:
ENGINE:
Four cylinders in line, iron block and head
Bore x stroke	84.1mm x 80mm
Capacity	1,778cc
Valvegear	Overhead-valve
Compression ratio	10.0:1
Fuelling	Twin SU carburettors
Maximum power	115bhp (SAE) at 6,000rpm
Maximum torque	112lb ft at 4,000rpm

TRANSMISSION:
Four-speed all-synchro with overdrive
Final drive ratio   4.56:1

WHEELS/TYRES:
Disc wheels with 165 SR15in tyres

BODYWORK: Two-door saloon only

WEIGHT   2,403lb (1,090kg)

PERFORMANCE: (Source: *Wheels*, 1968)
Max speed	104mph
0–50mph in top	7.7sec
30–50mph in top	8.0sec

intended to be, the two cars had perhaps more in common than would be expected. Not only did the two cars have the same 102.4in (2.6m) wheelbase, but their engines and gearboxes were also shared.

With the run up to the car's launch in September 1956 being so hectic, nobody had given consideration to a name for it. The Amason name was then chosen (which became the Amazon later on), but Kreidler, a small manufacturer of mopeds, took exception to this, claiming the trademark as theirs. After much negotiation, Volvo was allowed to use the Amazon badge on its new car, but only for the Swedish market. All exported cars were known as the 120 series and 220 series instead, the launch car being the 121. Despite this however, enthusiasts around the world have adopted the Amazon tag for the car.

Speculation about the car's specification was rife in the run up to its launch. Press reports talked about a car which would be powered by a six-cylinder engine and maybe even a development of the V8 seen in the Philip prototype. Sketchy details were released to the press in February 1956 but that only fuelled the fire. Announcements were made in April 1956 that the prototypes had been completed but the car was not going on sale until the following year. Immediately, the press started to talk about a 2.5-litre six-cylinder engine being developed, but when the 121 first went on sale it was equipped with a single-carb 1,583cc version of the three-bearing B14 engine fitted to the PV444. Badged the B16A and with just 60bhp on tap, performance was not exactly startling with part of the problem being the three-speed manual gearbox carried over from the PV444. What was really needed was an extra ratio, but the intended four-speed 'box was not ready at that stage.

At the front there were still coil springs and double wishbones, but the set-up was redesigned to have shorter upper and longer lower wishbones. There were also changes at the back, with the rear axle now located by longitudinal supports in rubber bushes in place of the angled support arms fitted previously. Torsional stiffness was excellent despite the large doors, and great attention was paid to high-quality rustproofing to ensure the bodyshell stayed in fine shape.

As soon as the car was shown to the public on 1–2 September 1956, orders came flooding in. Priced at SKr12,600, buyers were asked to pay a SKr4,000 deposit, with the first cars promised for delivery the following spring. In the event, the initial batches of cars were shipped in February and March 1957 and they were an instant success, despite costing a third more then the PV444L by this time. Problems soon arose however, with leaking bodies, self-lowering windows and rattling gear levers. Volvo acted swiftly to cure the problems and very soon the car was free of such irritations.

By the end of 1957, 5,000 Amazons had been built and in March 1958 the next development arrived – the 122S. First shown at the Geneva Motor Show, the B16B-engined 122S featured twin SU carbs and a reprofiled camshaft to raise power to 85bhp, an increase of nearly 50 per cent. An all-synchromesh four-speed gearbox was now available and to help the car handle better the ride height was lowered by an inch (25mm). The Motor tested a 122S and was astonished at how fast it was considering it packed just a 1.6-litre engine. A 0–60mph time of 17.8 seconds may seem sluggish by modern standards, but at the time it was remarkable for a large saloon. In fact, the first thing about the Amazon that made an impression on the road tester was its performance – after that it was fairly ordinary in most

Dropheads and coupés

Although Volvo did not officially turn out anything other than saloon and estate versions of the 120 series, some independent companies did try their hand at producing convertibles and coupés.

The first was by Danish Volvo dealer Ole Sommer in 1960. Using a shortened PV445 chassis, the car featured 120 series panels at the front end and a hand-made aluminium coupé rear end.

The Sommer car was a one-off, but Belgian coachbuilder Jacques Coune made five examples of his convertible, the first of which was shown at the 1963 Brussels Salon. Based on a two-door saloon, the Coune convertible cost 50 per cent more than the car on which it was based, thanks to a leather retrim, reworked doors and much body strengthening. One car was a two-seater while the other four were four-seaters.

By the time this view was taken in 1961, two-tone Amazons were the exception rather than the rule, with single-colour cars being far more commonplace.

respects. The driving position was seen as old-fashioned and once up to speed it lost some of the refinement which gave it an edge at lower velocities. Fuel consumption was also not especially competitive, but at least the car was comfortable, solidly built and very well equipped. That first test by *The Motor* marked the introduction of official UK sales with right-hand drive cars. Although the company did not have an especially strong image in Britain, its cars had received some coverage in British car magazines and sales began to increase steadily.

In September 1959, *Road & Track* compared a 122S with a PV444, a car which was at that time obsolete, but in many ways little changed from the PV544 which had superseded it. Considering this was the year of greatest excess when it came to American car design, *Road & Track*'s testers found the 122S refreshingly understated. There were no outrageous fins or huge slabs of chrome daubed across the car, merely clean lines and useful safety features. This was something that

was not lost on the magazine's reporters, who clearly felt that what Volvo was doing was far more worthwhile than the tactics of many American car producers. Interestingly, the 122S was a far more compact car than its competitors in the American marketplace, and when positioned alongside its European competitors the car was comparable in size – yet the Amazon compared favourably in whichever market it was being sold.

Within six months of the appearance of the 122S, seatbelts were fitted as standard to all 120 series cars, the first time that such a move was made by any car maker in the world. By the end of the year, all 120 series cars were also equipped with dual-circuit, servo-assisted brakes. Safety has always been high on Volvo's list of priorities – now it was being seen as the thing that Volvo stood for more than anything else. This braking system upgrade in November 1958 coincided with the first official Volvo imports into the UK. It was the Brooklands Motor Company which

The first Amazons were available as four-door saloons only, with Volvo's production facilities running flat-out to try to keep up with demand.

Few cars of the era had a padded dash but, with typical Volvo attention to detail, the Amazon had one, although there was still a long way to go before the interior was truly safe in an impact.

opened up and given its head. A standing quarter-mile time of 19 seconds was fast and he reckoned the Volvo was 'as fast and vivid as a rocket burst'. Indeed, the performance of the 122S was something that was at odds with its appearance, as when *The Motor* tested one in 1959, it described the car as 'a Swedish family saloon offering performance with a kick in it'.

Having launched the 120 series in Britain, the next step was to unleash it on the American public, so the car was unveiled at the New York Auto Show in April 1959. It was very warmly received, but when the first examples were sold soon after, it was clear that all was not well. The camshafts fitted to some engines had been badly made and very quickly everyone knew about it.

The common practice at that time was for car makers to deny everything and hope the problems would go away, but Volvo chose to announce very openly, that a mistake had been made and the company would put everything right without any owners losing out. This did much to bolster Volvo's caring image.

For the 1961 model year the seats were completely redesigned to give greater comfort and more interior space. The following year the 75bhp B18A and 90bhp B18D engines became available, having debuted in B18B form in the new P1800 coupé three months earlier. This was the first time the 1.8-litre engine was available in the Amazon, and instead of simply being a development of the earlier 1.6-litre unit, it was a new design with a five-bearing crankshaft and a new cylinder head which allowed easy tuning. At the same time there was also a move to 12-volt electrics and buyers who opted for the 90bhp Sports engine benefited from Girling disc brakes at the front.

The next major change for the Amazon range came in October 1961, when the two-door car was introduced. Known as the Type 131, at first it was only available in

handled the process, but a £923 pre-tax price translated into a very hefty £1,399 by the time duties had been paid. You had to want one very badly to pay that sort of money! Perhaps sales were helped along by Mike Hawthorn's review of the car, which appeared in an edition of the *Sunday Express* shortly before his death. In it, he extolled the virtues of the 122S, saying its staid looks and conservative Swedish image could all be forgiven when the car was

Above: The photograph may be obviously staged, but the message is clear. In Sweden, Volvo's cars were seen as one of the family.

Left: The 122S was the first truly sporty Amazon, although even the basic 1.6-litre single-carburettor version was surprisingly agile. The 122S was fitted with twin-carburettors, which were very effective at making the car more perky.

Right: The PV544 had led the Swedish charge in the 1950s, creating a very desirable image for the Volvo marque. The Amazon continued that, with the car enjoying a massive US following.

Gunnar Engellau

Although the Amazon had been developed before Gunnar Engellau took the helm of Volvo on 13 August 1956, it was due to his efforts and leadership that the company went from strength to strength throughout the 15 years that he led the car maker. One of the main reasons was his focus on the American market, the first US sales having taken place just the year before he took over at Volvo. Although just 50 cars had been shipped over in 1955, he increased this to 5,000 in 1956 and 10,300 in 1957. Each year the numbers increased and it was because of this that during his time as CEO of Volvo AB, Engellau saw turnover rise from SKr600m to SKr6,000m, with annual car production increasing from 31,000 to 205,000.

He handed over the reins to Pehr Gyllenhammar in 1971, but remained as Chairman of the Board until 1978. He died on 5 January 1980, aged 80.

Even with a 1.6-litre engine, the Amazon was blessed with good performance. By the time the larger units were fitted the car was a surprisingly sporty car.

Scandinavia. It was at this point that the Amazon name was dropped officially – except that right up until the end of production Volvo referred to the car as the Amazon in its advertisements! So when the estate version of the 120 series arrived in February 1962, there should not have been any references to the term Amazon, but in reality, the car became known as the Amazon P220 Combi. It had taken six years for the estate to appear, but this wasn't because of drawn-out development, it was simply a matter

Jan Wilsgaard

In 1950, Jan Wilsgaard was studying sculpture at art college in Gothenburg. He still had a year to go before his course would be complete, but instead of graduating he seized the chance to become Volvo's first full-time exterior designer in the styling department that the company was setting up that year. His first three designs, the Philip of 1950, the 1952 PV179 and the '55' of 1953 did not see production, but his fourth car, started in 1953, was the one which put Volvo on the map for many enthusiasts – the Amazon.

In his early days, Wilsgaard was often having to compete with independent styling houses, as there was not great confidence in Volvo's in-house styling department because it wasn't well enough established. It did not take long to become established though and Wilsgaard designed such icons as the Amazon and many of Volvo's concepts including the VESC (1972), New York Taxi (1976) and Volvo Concept Car (1980). He also designed the 144, 164, 200 series and the 700 series.

The last car to be designed with the involvement of Wilsgaard was the 850, launched in 1991. Continuing the boxy theme started in the 1960s with the 140, it was the last of the old-school Volvos before Peter Horbury arrived to inject some aesthetic appeal into the marque. Although Wilsgaard's angular styling may not be liked by everybody, his name lives on at Volvo as there's an annual scholarship awarded to hopeful students studying at the Gothenburg Institute of Arts and Crafts – and it carries his name.

of production capacity, as Volvo did not have enough space to build a two-door saloon alongside a four-door version as well as a five-door split-tailgate model.

The estate car would not have been ready for an early introduction anyway, as it was not just a saloon with a tweaked rear end. Although the cars were much the same as far back as the B-pillars, the rear doors were changed and the whole of the back of the car was new – even under the skin. The redesigned suspension was strengthened and lowered to allow a low floor which could hold nearly half a ton without giving problems. The tailgate was split to allow long loads to rest on the closed lower half with the top half open, and the car's practicality made it very popular. Alternatively, the car could be driven with the lower half of the tailgate open thanks to a top-hinged numberplate – the same idea that was used for the first Minis. Using this facility it was possible to carry an 8ft x 4ft (2.4m x 1.2m) sheet of wood – something which may not have been necessary very often, but which nothing else smaller than a van could do.

The only problem Volvo had was building enough cars to satisfy demand – a situation which was remedied by the building of more factories. The first overseas factory was opened in Canada, in June 1963, in Halifax, Nova Scotia. Less than two years later there was a factory at Ghent in Belgium but the production facility that made the biggest difference to Volvo's capacity was the opening of the Swedish Torslanda factory in 1964. This allowed up to 200,000 cars to be built each year, although it would be several years before that many cars would be made there – the first year's production tally was just 118,465 units, around half of which were sold in Sweden.

More improvements were promised to the Amazon range for 1965, the most significant of which was the introduction of front

Amazon identification

With numerous different badges and what would seem to be frequent identity crises, working out which Amazon is which isn't especially easy. Here is a quick-reference guide.

121 (B16A)

The first production model, built 1957–1961. 60bhp 1,582cc single-carb engine, four doors and three-speed manual gearbox.

122S (B16B)

Produced between 1958 and 1961, export models with an 85bhp twin-carb 1,582cc engine and four-speed gearbox.

121 (B18A)

Still just one carburettor, but new cylinder head and increase to 1,778cc means there's a choice of 75bhp or 85bhp. Built 1961–1968, there's a choice of two-door or four-door saloons, although the latter was dropped in 1967.

122S (B18D)

Twin-carburettor version of the 121, current 1961–1968 with four disc

brakes. Two-door available from 1963, last four-door built in 1967. Power outputs 90bhp, 95bhp or 100bhp.

221/222

Amazon estate, made 1962–1969; 1,778cc engine. Sometimes referred to as 121 or 221 Combi or estate.

123GT

115bhp version of 1778cc P1800 engine, two-doors. Made 1966–1968.

121 (B20A)

Two-door only, with B20A 1998cc engine as 140 series. Produced 1968–1970; 90bhp enough to give 100mph top speed.

122S (B20B)

Most powerful Amazon of all, last 122S model (1968–1970) has 118bhp 1,998cc powerplant normally seen in 140 series. Two-door only; can manage over 100mph.

disc brakes as standard. Estate versions also had servo assistance, and the sills were now partly galvanised to improve the cars' lifespan. Having led the way with standard front seatbelts the next step was to redesign the seats to ensure that passengers sat properly. Medical experts were consulted and as a result there were new fabrics, new designs, and new construction techniques, to make sure that accidents did not occur because drivers weren't sitting comfortably, or injuries sustained

were more severe than they might have been because passengers weren't properly located.

For 1966, the big news was the introduction of a more affordable Amazon. Known as the Favorit, the car was launched despite the similar attempt made with the PV444 having flopped and the car being with-drawn after just two seasons. That was probably because the Favorit was not nearly as stripped out as the PV444 Export had been, with equipment reductions con-fined to the external brightwork being removed, a slightly more austere interior and a three-speed all-synchromesh gearbox in place of the four-speed unit normally fitted.

By this stage, the Amazon was being built in large numbers and it looked as though the car would remain in production despite its supposed successor, the 140, going on sale in 1966. For 1967 a new sports version was unveiled. Badged the 123GT (or the 120GT in some export markets), the new car mated the 1.8-litre engine from the 1800S with the two-door bodyshell of the 122. With 115bhp on tap and a four-speed gearbox with overdrive, the car was more practical than the 1800S, as well as being more affordable.

At the end of 1967 the four-door Amazon was taken out of production, the 144 having become a more popular car although for the first half of the year the 121 was still the best-selling car in Sweden. The two-door and estate cars continued to be built and in Autumn 1968 it was announced that they would be available with the B20 2-litre engine – a bored-out version of the B18 powerplant. There was an increase in power to either 90bhp or 118bhp (SAE) depending on the state of tune, but the real benefit was the greatly improved torque. At the same time the cars were given the dual-circuit braking system that had been fitted to the 140 series from

the outset. The result of all this was a car which outperformed the 144 because of its lighter weight and high power output, and when the Australian magazine Wheels put a 122S through its paces in 1969, the testers were amazed at just how capable the car still was. Aged it may have been, but with excellent brakes, build quality, ride, refinement and comfort, the Amazon could still give its competitors a run for their money.

By the end of the 1960s, the Amazon had become a very familiar sight on the roads, especially in America. The earliest PV444s were two decades old, and many of them were still going strong. Already Volvo, which had been exporting cars for little more than a decade, had fostered a reputation for cars which lasted. To nurture this the company's advertising reinforced the stereotype with such slogans as: 'Tougher than dirt' and 'If you're undecided about buying a new Volvo, drive an old one'. The company even went so far as to rubbish its competitors' attempts to facelift their cars every year, stating proudly that its cars hardly changed from one year to another.

In 1969, the Amazon estate was discontinued, superseded by the 145 and leaving just the 122 in production. It was clear that the car would not be built for much longer, so changes for the 1970 model year

were very minor, restricted to front-seat headrests and the provision of rear seatbelts. It was now inevitable that Amazon production would stop soon after, and sure enough, in the summer of 1970, the last car was built. Bearing chassis number 667,323, the car was put into Volvo's museum.

Driving

One of the reasons why the 1800 coupé was hard to sell was because the Amazon offered as much performance but with much greater practicality. It might not look sporty but this is quite a wolf in sheep's clothing – at least when anything bigger than a 1.6-litre engine is fitted. Not only is it surprisingly perky, but it's also more refined and quieter than you would think.

The refinement comes partly from the car's bulk, which also helps it to ride smoothly, smothering the bumps as it seeks them out, but the trade-off for this is that the ride is also quite wallowy with a fair degree of roll in corners. Heavy understeer can feel disconcerting when the car is pushed hard, but it is completely predictable on the limit, to ensure that you don't come unstuck.

The cabin itself is pretty barren, especially on the earliest cars with vinyl seats, painted metal for most of the dash and no carpets on the floor. Later cars look no less austere but at least the seats are more comfortable as by this point Volvo had started to introduce orthopaedically designed

'55' – what might have been

Jan Wilsgaard's 1953 design study was hugely important to Volvo because it was this car which would become the PV544's replacement. Called the '55' in the studio, the car featured a profile very similar to the Amazon's, although much of the detail design such as the horse-collar grille, was shared with the Elizabeth prototype which had been built in 1953 – see Chapter 2. The car did not get beyond the full-size clay model, but elements of the design were used in the production Amazon.

The Amazon Combi, or estate, must surely rank as one of the most practical classic cars available, with its great durability and affordability.

Buying

1. Despite the oldest Amazons now approaching half a century on the road, rust isn't normally too much of a problem. Something that can turn an Amazon from a great example into a basket case is a leaking front or rear screen. So your first port of call should be the screen surrounds as once water starts to get in, it'll wreak havoc. The problem lies in the fact that using modern techniques to seal an Amazon screen aren't much use – old-fashioned mastic needs to be used to ensure the aperture stays watertight.

2. If the windscreen has been leaking it will be the corners of the bulkhead which will be the first to go – this is best checked from the engine bay. Also vulnerable are the walls of the footwells and to check the condition of these you will have to remove the cardboard trim panels.

3. The first area to corrode is normally the rear wheelarches, although serious rot is unlikely. The thing to look out for is poorly repaired rusted areas, as the wheel-arch lip is double-skinned and some repairers don't recreate the seam by the corner of the rear door.

4. While you're at the back of the car check the panels below the rear wings, which become covered in road dirt then rot from behind. If corrosion has advanced it may have attacked the chassis legs so it's worth checking from inside the boot just how much rust there is. While you're inspecting inside the boot, look for a rotten spare wheel well if the drain hole has become blocked and also examine the bottom edge of the boot lid, which is double-skinned and prone to rust.

5. The front wings may rust along with the lower edges of the doors, and while you're on your knees, check the underside of the doors. Also inspect the sills along their entire length as well as both front and rear wheelarches.

6. Amazon estates don't suffer from rotten spare wheel wells as the layout is different, but the split tailgate can corrode badly, so inspect both halves carefully. Condensation can seep under the rear side window seals, so check the metalwork below this seal to make sure it is intact.

7. The area behind the headlamp bowls fills with mud which rots out the bowl itself along with the wing. New wings can be bolted on and plastic bowls are available, so repair is not difficult. The bottom edge of the bonnet and the seams around the grille can also rust, but major corrosion is unlikely.

8. Although most of the exterior trim is either stainless steel or anodised aluminium, and hence immune to corrosion, the front and rear bumpers are heavy, chrome-plated affairs which are very expensive to repair or replace. Each unit consists of five parts, each of which is of thick steel, so if bent they are not easy to straighten out.

9. The rest of the brightwork does not give any problems, although replacing the aluminium strips at the base of the C-pillar is difficult because they are secured by fastenings behind the headlining. Even the mazak parts, which on most cars pit badly, don't corrode much on the Amazon because they are of much higher quality than is usual.

10. The Amazon's engine is as durable as its bodywork, with 150,000 miles easily attainable, as long as the unit is serviced properly. Because it is such an uncomplicated powerplant it is easy both to service and work on.

11. Three engines sizes were available, the most common being the 1,780cc B18 unit. The earlier 1,580cc B16 engine and the 1,990cc B20 that was used for the last of the cars are both relatively rare, but all three units are essentially the same.

12. Both the B18 and B20 engines are durable, racking up 200,000 miles quite happily as long as they have had regular oil changes. Make sure the oil filter is the correct Volvo item, complete with non-return valve as anything less will starve the bearings of oil when starting from cold. If there's a thump like worn big-end bearings at cruising speed, it is probably because the timing gears have worn.

13. Although the engines aren't frugal, especially heavy fuel consumption is probably due to a faulty thermostat, allowing the engine to run cool. Oil pressure should be around 40psi at idle once the engine has warmed up, while 50–55psi should be on the clock once the car is on the move.

14. Amazon transmissions are amazingly durable, whichever unit is fitted. Although three-speed manual or automatic gearboxes will be found on some cars, the chances are you will be looking at a four-speed unit either with or without overdrive. The overdrive unit is well worth having, but even if the car you're looking at doesn't have one, upgrading the gearbox isn't difficult.

15. The front suspension is straightforward, being of a double wishbone design which requires little in the way of maintenance. Apart from bushes wearing, there's hardly anything to check.

16. On post-1966 cars, the rear suspension is equally problem-free, this using a twin-trailing arm design. Earlier Amazons featured a single radius arm of uncharacteristically poor design and being of pressed steel they rust badly, although most cars have had replacements fitted by now.

17. Estates have a problem of their own with the rear suspension, because their much more heavy-weight radius arms contain very large rubber and aluminium bushes. Because of the higher potential loadings on these cars due to the greater weight, the arms can crack under the strain.

seats. 'Due to the high seating position and adjustability of front seats both for rake and fore-and-aft position, driving the Amazon should be pleasant for almost anyone' *Track & Traffic* stated in its 1962 test of a 121. Since then, expectations have increased somewhat, but it is true of the later cars – less so of the first ones off the production lines.

Tuning and modifying

The solid build of an Amazon means durability isn't compromised, but performance is not as good as it could be – which is why it's worth squeezing a bit more power out of the engine. The great thing about the Amazon's powerplants is that they are easy to tune and reliability is not compromised as a result. The rule is that a 121 has a single SU carburettor while a 122 or a 123 has a pair of carbs. So if you have a 121 the easiest thing to do is to fit a pair of SUs along with a standard 122 manifold to see an increase in power from 85bhp to around 100bhp.

To help the engine breathe more freely it is also worth fitting a more free-flowing exhaust manifold – a 2in system in place of the rather restricted standard item. Once this has been done it is worth investing in a slightly less tame camshaft, especially if you're working on a single carburettor car. These were equipped with an A-specification camshaft while those fitted to the twin-carb cars featured a C-specification unit, but neither of these is as good as the D-specification item with which the GT was equipped. Fitting one of these hotter camshafts will see the power output rise to somewhere near the 120bhp mark without sacrificing tractability or reliability. In fact, at this stage the engine is so far from its limits that durability isn't remotely compromised.

The next stop is the ignition system, which benefits from being converted to an electronic one in place of the standard points and condenser. There are two routes to this, the first being the fitment of an aftermarket set-up. If you don't want to take this route the alternative is to fit the Bosch system from a post-1975 240, complete with distributor, control box, coil, ballast resistor and wiring harness.

Having upped the power, the next step is to improve the Amazon's handling by fitting better dampers. The preferred option is generally Bilstein units, which give excellent handling and last pretty much forever – it's not unknown for a quarter of a million miles to be racked up on a set. While the dampers are being replaced it is also worth replacing the original coil springs with units that are an inch shorter. These allow the car to sit a little bit lower and also sharpen up the handling thanks to the slightly lower centre of gravity. Having gone to all this trouble it's worth replacing the original Metalastik bushes with polyurethane ones which are less prone to perishing and which also give a slightly firmer ride.

Because the Standard Amazon

brakes are pretty good, there is not much required to help them cope with the extra power. Until 1965 some Amazons were fitted with drum brakes at the front, so fitting the disc system that was installed from that year is a worthwhile and easy option. Harder pads are useful, the normal recommendation being Mintex 1155 units, although Mintex 1144 items can be fitted if a warm up period will be available to get the brakes up to temperature; if the car is going to be driven really hard the dust shields can be removed to help dissipate the heat. There's not that much you can do with the rear brakes, although they're not bad anyway. Riveted instead of bonded shoes is a good idea just to make sure that if things get really hot the shoes aren't going to start falling apart. A servo is also a worthwhile fitment, because many Amazons weren't equipped with one. This won't make the brakes any more effective, but it will help you to pull the car up more easily thanks to lower pedal pressures.

All these modifications assume you are after reliable power for fast road use and perhaps the odd excursion on to the track. If the car is being prepared for rallying there are extra steps available to make the car more

reliable. By boring the engine out to 2.1 litres it's possible to increase torque figures while the fitting of an 1800E cylinder head (which was also fitted to the last of the 140s) allows the engine to breathe more easily. If reliability is paramount it is worth fitting a 1¾in SU in place of the normally preferred twin SUs. This means you do not have to worry about keeping the carburettors balanced, but it doesn't sacrifice too much power.

The final option is to go for the ultimate road car with the most powerful engine possible. That means sourcing a late B20 engine that would have originally been installed in a 1970–1973 140. These engines have eight bolts securing the flywheel instead of the six bolts seen on earlier cars and in standard form they offer 130bhp and 130lb ft of torque. But, by boring them out to 2.1 litres and fitting a pair of SU or Weber carburettors it is easy to get closer to 180bhp.

One of the most popular modifications that owners make to their Amazons is the fitment of 5.5in wheels in place of the standard 4.5in units. This in turn allows the fitment of 195/70 tyres to improve grip and roadholding.

Left: The 123GT matched the 115bhp 1.8-litre engine of the 1800S with the practicality of the Amazon's two-door bodyshell, and was quite a hot rod.

Right: This is one of the later Duetts, with its single-piece windscreen. The Amazon may be newer, but it's no more charming than its predecessor.

Tuned Amazons

Ever since its introduction, the Amazon had been seen as a sporting saloon thanks to its predictable handling and sprightly performance. So it was a natural contender for the attentions of tuners who wanted to make it go even faster without having to sacrifice the car's usability. Not only that, but a choice of different body styles meant buyers could have a sporting coupé, saloon or even estate without the need to resort to special bodywork. As a result, some British police forces ran tuned Amazons knowing that they would keep running while still being able to keep up with villains who were using increasingly fast cars in attempts to get away.

Perhaps the best-known of the Amazon tuners was Ken Rudd who, having hung up his racing helmet, devoted himself to making cars go faster, especially the Amazon. He offered upgrades for saloons, coupés and estates at a time when estates were seen as nothing other than utilitarian workhorses. By focusing on allowing the cylinder head to breathe better, along with fitting spicier camshafts, uprated valve springs and tweaked carburation, Ken Rudd was able to build Amazons that really flew.

When *Autosport* tested a Ruddspeed 121 in 1964 they were glowing in their praise, claiming it was a truly sporty drive but one which gave away nothing in terms of practicality. A

ride height lowered by 1½in (37mm) allowed the Amazon to stay composed when taken by the scruff of the neck. A fabricated tubular manifold and exhaust system meant it sounded as good as it went. A polished and gas-flowed cylinder head enabled the powerplant to develop 108bhp at 6,000rpm which

In an age when tarmac-tearing saloons and estates were the preserve of specialist tuners, Ken Rudd was the best-known of all the Volvo experts to liberate extra power for the Amazon.

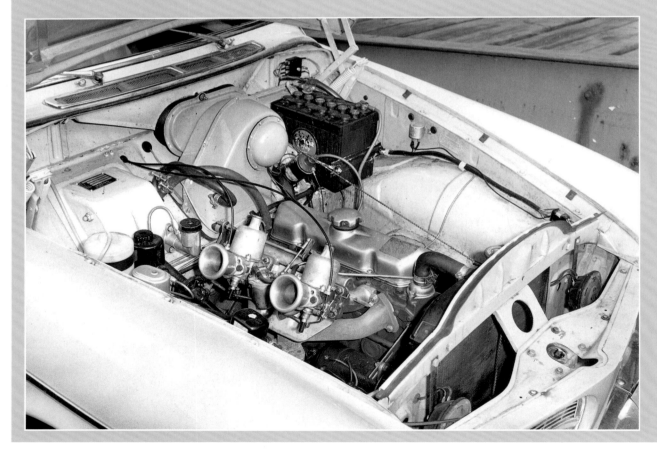

was enough to push the car to a top speed of 107mph (172kph). Not only that but the standing quarter-mile could be despatched in just under 18 seconds – incredibly quick for a four-door saloon which could carry five adults in comfort.

Later that year, *Autocar* put a Ruddspeed Volvo estate through its paces and came away equally impressed. Offering 118bhp thanks to a wilder camshaft, twin SU carburettors, a more free-flowing exhaust and a modified cylinder head, the Ruddspeed car was able to sprint from rest to 60mph (96kph) in just 12.2 seconds – a year earlier the same road testers had clocked a standard car at 21.1 seconds. Similarly, the 60–80mph (96–129kph) time in top gear was slashed from 22.5 seconds to just 10.9 seconds,

which meant Ruddspeed was offering something to British car buyers which, at the time, was more or less unique – an affordable and reliable performance estate.

But it wasn't only Ruddspeed which offered faster Amazons, as Robert Bodle of Oxfordshire-based Dorchester Service Station was also selling them. A modified cylinder head, raised compression ratio, special valve springs which permitted 6,800rpm and reprofiled manifolds produced a car which was capable of 102mph (164kph). Not only that, but the 0–60mph time was reduced to just 12 seconds while fuel economy improved thanks to the greater efficiency of the tweaked engine.

Meanwhile, in South Africa, a company named Alconi was busy

Although most of the Amazons converted by Ken Rudd were civilian road cars, the significant extra power meant they were just the ticket for police forces wanting speed with reliability.

making Amazons go faster. Better exhausts, ported and polished cylinder heads, larger valves and different carburettor needles gave power outputs of up to 135bhp, while also allowing the powerplant to run more cleanly and economically. With a top speed of 110mph (177kph) the cars also benefited from uprated brake pads and stiffer suspension.

Left: In the 1960s, many of
Sweden's roads were still unmetalled,
but that made little difference with
the Amazon, because it was so
ruggedly built.

Below: Volvos may have had a
reputation for being ponderous to
drive, but that's really based on the
looks of the later cars. In reality, the
Amazon was actually not at all bad
dynamically.

P1900, P1800 *and* 1800ES

In 1953, Assar Gabrielsson visited America, and he saw how popular European sports cars from Jaguar and MG had become. Triumph and Austin-Healey were about to repeat the feat and he decided that Volvo should have a slice of the action. Until that point he had had no desire to build a sporting car – he had no qualms about his company's cars being strictly functional.

The turning point was to come when he visited Chevrolet's factory in Flint, Michigan, which was about to go into production with the glassfibre Corvette. The material was cheap and easy to work with, and with so little tooling needed to enter production it seemed like a neat solution to his problem of a lack of production capacity. He then paid a visit to California-based Glasspar, which had pioneered the use of glassfibre for boat construction and had already started to have some success in the production of cars with this fashionable composite, and his mind was made up. Gabrielsson commissioned Glasspar to design, engineer and build a glassfibre bodyshell to mount on a separate chassis.

Bill Tritt, founder of Glasspar, produced the designs and a chassis was developed to take PV444 running gear, using that car's 1.4-litre B14 engine and three-speed gearbox. A pair of SU carburettors was installed to increase power to 70bhp and the powerplant had the B14B tag bestowed upon it.

Glasspar was to build the first 20 bodies with assembly then being transferred to Volvo. By June 1954, the first cars were being shown to the public, provisionally called the Volvo P1900, but already changes had been made. Most significant was its transformation from fixed-head coupé to roadster with detachable hardtop – no retractable hood of any kind was fitted. One of the reasons for these last-minute changes was that Volvo's

chief designer, Jan Wilsgaard, had not been consulted at all about the P1900's lines, and he had serious reservations about some elements of the transatlantic styling. So, while he tidied up the exterior design he also

Volvo had gained an enviable reputation for building durable cars by the time the P1900 was launched, but the car did little to bolster that image.

P1800 coupé with B18B engine
1961–1968

ENGINE:
Four cylinders in line, iron block and head	
Bore x stroke	84.1mm x 80mm
Capacity	1,780cc
Valvegear	Overhead valve
Compression ratio	9.5:1
Fuelling	Twin SU HS6
Maximum power	100bhp (SAE) at 5,500rpm (1961–1963)
	108bhp (SAE) at 5,800rpm (1963–1965)
	115bhp (SAE) at 6,000rpm (1965–1968)
Maximum torque	108lb ft at 4,000rpm

TRANSMISSION:
Rear-wheel-drive; Four-speed all-synchromesh
Overdrive optional 1961–1963, standard
1963–1968
(But all UK 1800s were fitted with overdrive as standard)
Final drive ratio	4.1:1 (without overdrive)
	4.56:1 (with overdrive)

SUSPENSION:
Front: Independent with coil springs, telescopic dampers, wishbones, anti-roll bar
Rear: Live axle, coil springs, telescopic dampers, Panhard rod

STEERING:
Cam and roller, unassisted
Turns lock-to-lock	3.25

BRAKES:
Front: Disc	Rear: drum

Girling servo assistance

WHEELS/TYRES:
Pressed-steel wheels with 165 x 15in Pirelli Cinturato tyres

BODYWORK:
Two-door coupé of monocoque construction

DIMENSIONS:
Length	14ft 5in (4.39m)
Wheelbase	8ft 0in (2.44m)
Track	4ft 4in (1.32m)
Width	5ft 7in (1.7m)
Height	4ft 2in (1.27m)

WEIGHT: 2,400lb (1,090kg)

PERFORMANCE: (Source: *The Autocar*)
Max speed	104mph
0–60mph	13.2sec
30–50mph in top	8.3sec (not overdrive top)
50–70mph in top	9.3sec (14.8sec overdrive top)

PRICE WHEN NEW:
UK £1,836 12s 9d (July 1962)
USA $3,940 (November 1961)

NUMBER MADE:
1800 coupé (all types)	39,407
P1800	6,000

1800S with B20B engine
1968–1969

As P1800 except:
ENGINE:
Bore x stroke	88.9mm x 80mm
Capacity	1,986cc
Fuelling	Twin Zenith-Stromberg carburettors (LHD cars)
	Twin SU HS6 carburettors (RHD cars)
Maximum power	118bhp at 5,800rpm (SAE)
Maximum torque	123lb ft at 3,500rpm

TRANSMISSION:
Final drive ratio	4.3:1

BRAKES:
Now with dual-circuit hydraulics

PERFORMANCE: (Source: *Volvo*)
Max speed	110mph

PRICE WHEN NEW:
UK £1,814 1s 3d (July 1966)
USA $4,280 (August 1966)

NUMBER MADE:
1800S (total)	23,993
B (1963)	2,000
D (1963–1964)	4,500
E (1964–1965)	4,000
F (1965–1966)	4,500
M (1966–1967)	4,500
P (1967–1968)	2,800
S (1968–1969)	1,693

P1800E coupé with B20E engine
1969–1972

Also with B20F engine for North American market 1971–1972
As B20B-engined P1800 except:

ENGINE:
Compression ratio	10.5:1
Fuelling	Bosch electronic fuel injection
	Maximum power
B20E:	130bhp at 6,000rpm (SAE)
B20F:	125bhp at 6,000rpm (SAE)
Maximum torque	
B20E:	130lb ft at 3,500rpm
B20F:	123lb ft at 3,500rpm

TRANSMISSION:
Optional three-speed Borg-Warner 35 automatic transmission
Final drive ratio:	3.91:1

BRAKES:
Front & Rear:	Disc

WHEELS/TYRES:
Cast alloy with steel rims (1969–1971), pressed steel disc wheels (1971–1972), fitted with 185/70HR tyres.

WEIGHT: 2,533lb (1,150kg)

PERFORMANCE: (Source: *Motor*)
Max speed	112mph
0–60mph	9.6sec
30–50mph in top	11.0sec (overdrive top)
50–70mph in top	12.2sec (overdrive top)

PRICE WHEN NEW:
UK £2,254 7s 6d (August 1970)
USA $4,595 (February 1970)

NUMBER MADE:
1800E (total)	9,414
T (1969–1970)	2,799
U (1970–1971)	4,750
W (1971–1972)	1,865

1800ES with B20E/B20F engine
1971–1973

As 1972 1800E except:
ENGINE:
Max power: 112bhp at 6,000rpm (SAE) on US cars

DIMENSIONS:
Length	14ft 5in (4.39m)

WEIGHT: 2,621lb (1,190kg)

PERFORMANCE:
(Source: *Motor*)
Max speed	112mph
0–60mph	9.7sec
30–50mph in top	12.0sec (overdrive top)
50–70mph in top	12.8sec (overdrive top)

UK PRICE WHEN NEW (March 1972):
£2,650.62

NUMBER MADE:
1800ES (total)	8,077
W (1971–1972)	3,070
Y (1972–1973)	5,007

Who designed the 1800?

Although Pietro Frua is widely credited with styling the 1800 during his days with Ghia, there's much more to who was behind the final designs. Gunnar Engellau tasked Helmer Petterson in 1957 to find an Italian styling house to come up with some designs for a successor to the ill-fated P1900.

It just so happened that Petterson's 23-year-old son Pelle was studying industrial design in the USA, and his father was keen to launch him into automotive design. He took the opportunity of asking his son to produce some designs for a new Volvo sports coupé, which he then presented to the designers at Ghia.

As a result, Pelle started working for Ghia, but problems soon arose when Volkswagen commissioned Ghia to develop a new sports coupé from them, in conjunction with Karmann. The outcome was that Pelle and the whole project was moved to Frua, also based in Turin, to complete.

By the summer of 1957, there were five designs from which to choose, and these were presented to Gunnar Engellau. Two were by Carrozzeria Ghia, a pair had come from Frua and one was by Pelle Petterson. When Engellau chose Petterson's designs he was not at all happy that he had been duped, but it was agreed that Petterson junior would work for Frua, which would see the designs through to production and build the first prototype cars as well.

Right top: The first P1900 prototypes did not have a hood of any sort, being fitted instead with just a removable hard top. That was clearly impractical, so a hood mechanism was devised later.

Right bottom: Volvo's first sports car was quite an attractive vehicle, with the new technology of glassfibre used to reduce construction costs. The car was still too expensive to build however.

Below: This is one of the first P1800 prototypes, and it barely differs from the production version which was shown in 1960. Its lines still looked good a decade later.

turned his hand to the interior, styling a new dash which was more European in design.

From the outset it was clear that sales would be low, so there was little money available to develop the separate chassis. The solution was to build a tubular frame to which were mounted the suspension, steering, engine and transmission of the PV444. To keep weight down and maximise space there was no spare wheel – Volvo had the utmost faith in the latest Scandinavian Trelleborg tyres with which the car was equipped, the claim being that they were puncture-proof.

Having made its debut in September 1954 – and still without a name, although Volvo Sport had been suggested – Volvo announced that the car would be going into production later that autumn, at the rate of one each day. There was talk of an initial batch of 300 cars being available, and to generate interest in

the car a trio of 1900s set off around the country, visiting all the Volvo dealers.

The lack of a folding roof was bad news for many potential buyers – they did not like the idea of just a detachable (and non-stowable) hard top. Thorough testing took place in 1955 and in March 1956 a re-engineered P1900 was taken on a 10,000-mile (16,000km) tour of Southern Europe and North Africa. Although it was reported as running smoothly, it didn't. All sorts of build-quality problems were apparent, but soon after the car arrived back in Sweden the first customer cars were delivered. Only 44 were built in 1956. The following year was even worse with just 23 P1900s produced and it was pretty clear that the car was never going to make any money.

Hand-built bodyshells meant high production costs and glassfibre, which was in its infancy, meant production standards weren't as

high as Volvo wanted. The car was shown at the 1956 Earls Court Motor Show, but a price tag of £2,100 (inflated by import duty and purchase tax) meant the car was more expensive than Jaguar's XK140 and more than double the price of an MGA. One weekend Assar Gabrielsson borrowed a P1900 to try it out and was so appalled with the quality of construction that when he returned to work on the Monday morning production was stopped

The 'juke-box' dash of pre-1968 1800s featured a turned aluminium effect, with the instruments set in individual nascelles. It was clearly American-inspired.

British expertise

Jensen's assembly of the P1800 and Pressed Steel's construction of the bodyshells was only the beginning of a huge amount of British content in the car. Around half of the components used in manufacture were of British origin. The benefits of this were manifold – sending parts direct to Jensen reduced production costs, it was clearly good for British industry, and the duty payable was also reduced, helping to keep purchase costs down.

When the P1800 was launched, it counted for much that the car featured parts supplied by world-renowned British companies seen as the leaders in their field. That's why brakes were supplied by Girling – discs for the front and drums for the rear and a de Normanville overdrive was fitted to all 1800s, the first time that a Swedish car had been fitted with a UK-supplied overdrive unit. Hardy-Spicer supplied the propshaft and there were dozens of small companies providing detail parts such as Birmingham-based Joseph Fray which manufactured much of the P1800's brightwork.

Although Volvo's relationship with Jensen wasn't without its quality problems, there was no shortage of British companies who supplied parts for the car which were well up to the standards expected by the Swedish company.

there and then. If the car could not be built to a standard worthy of the Volvo name, despite already costing more than most buyers were prepared to pay, there was no option but to pull the plug.

Assar Gabrielsson retired in 1956, and despite the spectacular lack of success of the P1900, his successor decided to pursue the goal of producing a Volvo sports car. It was Gunnar Engellau who had taken over the helm at Volvo, and he decided to embark on a new project. In 1957 Ghia was briefed to come up with designs for a two-plus-two sports coupé based on a shortened 120 series platform and the task was given to Pietro Frua, who was Ghia's chief stylist at the time. But before he completed the job he left Ghia to

set up his own design studio. Although he is generally credited with producing the final shape of the P1800, it is not as clear-cut as that – see separate sidebar for more details.

The design was one thing – production was another. Volvo had nowhere to build the car as its factory in the Swedish town of Olofstrom had no spare capacity and the Torslanda factory was not completed. Italy was ruled out but Germany threw up a couple of possibilities including Karmann. Having encountered problems with getting Ghia to produce designs for the car thanks to its working on a coupé for VW, it was predictable that the Karmann-Ghia project for the Wolfsburg company should also

scupper Volvo's production plans. VW was Karmann's biggest customer and it complained when the contract with Volvo was suggested, so there was no option but to look elsewhere.

A solution was found when the Pressed Steel Company signed a contract to produce the P1800 bodyshell for Volvo at its Linwood factory in Scotland. Also, to take the pressure off Volvo having to produce the car at all, a deal was reached with Jensen for the company to build the first 10,000 cars at its West Bromwich factory – all Volvo would have to do was supply the running gear, sourced from the Amazon.

By May 1959, the first official pictures of the P1800 (the 'P' stood

Robert Cumberford's V8 P1800

Ever since the first P1800 had seen the light of day it was clear that this was a sports coupé that wasn't really that sporting. More power was needed, and lots more torque, so the obvious answer was to fit a bigger engine.

Enter Robert Cumberford, whose original intention had been to market a V8-engined 1800S in America – the land of the V8, where there's no substitute for cubic inches. The powerplant chosen was Ford's '289' – a 4.7-litre unit rated at 196bhp (SAE) at 4,400rpm, thus offering a useful increase over the standard car's 100bhp or so.

It was a neat plan, as Volvo was struggling to build enough engines because it was short of production capacity. Ford on the other hand had no shortage of powerplants to sell, so a three-way arrangement was made between Cumberford, Ford and Volvo to build a prototype V8-engined 1800S.

The aim was to ensure that everything looked as though it had been done in the factory – this was not

meant to look like a home-produced hot rod, but that was easier said than done. Slotting the V8 into the engine bay, hooking it up to Ford's then-new C-4 automatic gearbox and not upsetting the car's balance was going to take some ingenuity. The answer was to position the engine well back as short of extending the car's nose by several inches there was no other way this could be done. This meant the engine and gearbox were sharing cabin space with the car's occupants, but at least only 20lb (9kg) of the car's 240lb (109kg) weight gain was over the front axle.

Having made everything fit, the next problem was sorting out the horrendous noise, heat and lack of refinement that was all-pervading in the cabin. After months of development both Volvo and Ford were happy that the car was now ready for sale, but it wasn't to be. Cumberford maintains that the reason for the plug being pulled was one of professional pride – putting the car he developed into the showrooms would effectively

be an admission that not only was the engine normally fitted to the 1800 not up to the job, but Volvo's own engineers weren't capable of engineering a replacement for it.

Or, perhaps it's because when Gunnar Engellau tried the prototype he was worried about just how powerful the car was. When introduced to the car he thought he was trying out an automatic 1800 – he wasn't told about the V8 engine under the bonnet. So when he floored the throttle to test out the acceleration and fishtailed madly from a standing start it was clear that the transmission wasn't the only thing that had been changed. He returned soon after with the car under control and was asked what he thought of it. At that stage he still did not know what had been done, but it was clear that the modifications were pretty major. 'I hope he knows dat woids his varranty' he responded, deadpan.

After the fiasco of the P1900, Volvo had to make sure that its next attempt at building a sports car was more successful. Working with Jensen did little to facilitate that.

for *Personvagn* or Personal car) were released, but it was not until January of the following year that the car was first seen in the metal, when it was unveiled at the Brussels Motor Show. Its American debut followed three months later at the New York Auto Show and just over a year later, in May 1961, the car went on sale in Sweden.

Even before the car was on sale, cracks had started to appear in the production agreements, with major rectification work having to be carried out on the bodyshells which were being produced at Linwood. The first 250 cars (destined for Swedish customers) were shipped to Gothenberg in 1961 but the quality was far short of what Volvo expected, with poor paint and sub-standard sealing.

Despite all the production

problems however, the press warmed to the car overall – sure, they did not think it was great in every respect, but they did accept that it offered a relatively small number of buyers something they could not find elsewhere, at least not for the money. 'The 1800 is a very civilised touring car for people who want to travel rapidly in style, at a price that many people who cannot afford a Ferrari or Aston Martin will be able to pay', commented *Road & Track*.

In July 1961, *The Autocar* presented an analysis of the P1800, in which they claimed that production would be wound up to 150 cars a day. That would have meant nearly 40,000 cars would roll off the production lines each year – but only around that number of cars was produced in total after a decade of production. Indeed, by the time the magazine's road

testers had got their hands on a P1800, a mere 400 cars had been built, yet production had been in progress for four months.

In October of the same year, the P1800 arrived in British showrooms, by which time, Jaguar's E-type had been unveiled and it was not that much more expensive than Volvo's offering. A great badge, fantastic performance and excellent dynamics put the P1800 in the shade, which didn't make the car any easier to sell. The area where the Volvo scored most highly was its grand touring capabilities – this was a car built for relaxed high-speed cruising rather than twisty back roads. As this was at odds with Volvo's reputation many car buyers did not equate the company with sports cars, although the reliability and durability that were synonymous with the Swedish marque didn't do any harm when it came to persuading potential customers to sign on the dotted line.

When *The Autocar* tested the car in the summer of 1962 its testers were impressed by the car's all-round ability, but it was clear that unless style was your main priority the car was beaten in just about every respect – and especially value – by Volvo's own 122 saloon. This offered more space, as much performance in day-to-day driving and a not especially inferior driving experience. But road testers being what they are, money was no object of course, and they happily lapped up the slick gearchange, reassuring brakes and confidence-inspiring roadholding.

The writers at *Car & Driver* were less equivocal about the P1800 when they tested it in September 1961 – they reckoned the ones who had got in first had got themselves

a bargain, but it wasn't just the great driving experience that made the car so good, it was its unbeatable value at $3,800. Or, as they put it: 'Until the P1800 came along, attractive 2/4 seater coupés capable of over 100mph were scarce unless the buyer was able to pay $4,000 and up (usually very up).'

Certainly the car was doing great things for Volvo's image in the USA – until its appearance, Volvo had been languishing in tenth slot in the imports league table. As soon as the 1800 went on sale the company's placings immediately improved, it becoming the sixth favourite importer. However, by the end of the decade even this figure would pale into insignificance, as Volvo would rise to number two, beaten only by Volkswagen.

Throughout 1961 and 1962, production continued, albeit at a rate somewhat short of what had

In 1968, the arrival of the 1800E brought with it a new dashboard that was more subdued than the previous offering.

originally been expected. The quality of the bodyshells being sent from Pressed Steel to Jensen wasn't good – in fact, the workers at Jensen were having to put right the bodywork before they could start on their own job of assembling the finished cars. Although the cars were not that much of an embarrassment by the time they reached the factory gates, it was hardly the most efficient method of producing cars.

As a result, in March 1963, Jensen produced its last P1800, after just 6,000 cars had rolled off its production lines. Volvo had terminated the contract, deciding to cut its losses and transfer assembly to its own Lundby plant in Sweden. Quality still hadn't been up to scratch, despite it having installed inspectors in Jensen's factory to ensure that standards improved. Although Jensen was no longer involved in the production process,

The later 1800 was fitted with straight bumpers all round, in place of the more characterful 'cow-horn' type fitted to earlier cars.

Convertible P1800s

Because the P1800 was based on a shortened 120 series floorpan, a drophead wasn't possible – at least not without extensive re-engineering. Doing such a thing would require a great deal of hand-building, and is something that would only be suitable for somebody offering a bespoke service.

Just such a person was Harold Radford who, in March 1965, produced a single convertible 1800S for a Hull-based Volvo dealer – not a pair, as is widely believed. Based on chassis 14459, it wasn't registered until early 1968, when it acquired the number 8888N. Over the next 14 years it covered over 100,000 miles (160,000km) in the hands of two owners before being abandoned in a barn, riddled with rust. It has now been completely restored and in the meantime at least one other car has

had its roof removed by an owner, after the car was rolled.

As well as the Radford convertible, around 50 1800s were converted by Long Island-based Volvo dealer Volvoville – the same dealership that supplied Irv Gordon with his 2 million-mile car.

Apart from Harold Radford (who created just one open 1800), US Volvo dealer Volvoville created drop-top versions of the 1800.

In 1965, Italian styling house Fissore came up with this proposal for a fastback version of the 1800. It's an attractive car, but the 1800ES was to prove even more practical without losing anything in terms of sporty appeal.

If you wanted a sporting estate at the end of the 1960s, there was little alternative to Volvo's 1800ES, unless you opted for Reliant's Scimitar GTE.

there was still a major British interest in the car's production, as bodies continued to be constructed by Pressed Steel at Linwood.

Once production had moved to Sweden the decision was made to make some changes to the P1800. It was rebadged to become the 1800S (for Sweden) and a more powerful version of the B18B engine was fitted, offering 108bhp thanks to a higher compression ratio and a racier camshaft – enough to raise the top speed to 110mph (177kph). There were also some specification changes, the most obvious being the adoption of standard 120 series wheels in place of the unique 1800-only wheel trims, and the adoption of leather trim for the seats.

Despite the 1800 being old-fashioned when it was introduced, British buyers continued to snap them up throughout the 1960s – the UK

was the second biggest export market for the car, beaten only by the USA, which bought half of the P1800s produced. Perhaps it was because the Swedes were less style-conscious, but in its homeland the P1800 never had anything more than a lukewarm reception, the locals preferring the cheaper, more practical and equally dynamic Amazon.

As the decade progressed, Volvo made a few changes here and there, most of them to reduce the amount of chrome trim. The now sought-after cowhorn bumpers were replaced with less unusual straight items in 1965, and in the previous year, more comfortable seats were installed while overdrive became standard for all 1800s, whatever the market. In 1966 some tweaks to the exhaust ports liberated a bit more power, 115bhp now being available, and the following season the curved

chrome flash which spanned most of the length of the car disappeared. Apart from these minor mods there was surprisingly little development of the 1800 throughout the decade.

It wasn't until 1968 that anything of any real significance occurred in terms of P1800 development, when the 1,780cc B18 engine in the 1800S was replaced with the torquier and more powerful B20 1,986cc unit. Pushing out 118bhp, the car's top speed did not increase, but the extra torque (now 123lb ft) meant the car was more relaxing to drive. Despite the capacity of the engine having increased to 2 litres, it retained the 1800S tag.

In 1968, the Linwood plant had been sold off to the Rootes Group, meaning a new factory had to be found for the 1800 bodyshells. Volvo seized the opportunity to break the link with Pressed Steel, and over the winter of 1968/69 the 1800's tooling was moved to Sweden, ready for the first all-Swedish cars. Once production had settled down, in August 1969, it was time to introduce the T series car, the big news for which was the abandoning of carburettors in favour of Bosch electronic fuel injection. In the process, the car's designation was changed from 1800S to 1800E, the 'E' standing for E*inspritz* – German for fuel injection.

The engine also featured a hotter camshaft and with larger valves and a higher compression ratio there was a healthy 130bhp on tap and a very useful 130lb ft of torque. But it wasn't just the mechanicals that were freshened up, as the cabin received a new ventilation system, there was a new matt-black grille and the dash received a complete overhaul with the old capillary-style instruments being junked in favour of more conventional dials. Yet despite the attention paid to the engine, the performance of the car was not significantly better than the versions which had preceded it. *Motor* managed to wind their car up to just 108mph (174kph), although a top

speed of closer to 120mph (193kph) was logged by testers writing for overseas magazines.

The worst year for sales since production began was 1968/69: Volvo managed to shift just 1,693 cars. Despite the car's age, the 1800 became much easier to sell when, in 1971, an automatic gearbox became available, especially in Volvo's biggest export market, the USA. In 1969/70, sales grew healthily to 2,799 but the following year things went even better with 4,750 cars sold – not huge numbers, but the fact that demand was increasing for such an outdated car showed that there was a loyal following.

By 1972, the 1800 coupé was too long in the tooth for Volvo to continue with production. Having been conceived nearly 15 years previously, it had been outclassed by a new generation of coupés which offered better packaging, dynamics and refinement for less money – by now Volvo's offering, at £2,300, was too expensive for comfort. So, on 22 June 1972, the last 1800E rolled off the production line after nearly 40,000 cars had been produced. The final cars, now known as Series W models, were fitted with improved seats, a matt-black plastic grille and tinted glass. A few more horses were coaxed out of the engine, with 135bhp on offer for European examples, but emission controls meant that the US-market 2-litre engine generated just 125bhp.

The demise of the 1800E did not mean it was the end of the line completely, as in Summer 1971 Volvo had launched an estate version of the 1800, the 1800ES. Using the same concept as Reliant's Scimitar GTE, which had been unveiled at the 1968 London Motor Show, the car gave the 1800 a new lease of life – even if it was for just an extra two years.

Until the launch of Radford's shooting-brake conversions of the Aston Martin DB5 in 1964, most estate cars were seen as practical boxes on wheels designed to ferry

people or goods around, and combining such utilitarianism with a sports car seemed absurd – but it was a concept which was to prove very popular when Reliant launched its Scimitar GTE. Volvo wanted a slice of the action, but it had been looking at the possibility of an estate-bodied 1800 well before the wraps were taken off the British car.

Fissore's proposals in 1965 for a fastback 1800 had sown the seeds of an idea, so Volvo approached Sergio Coggiola to produce some designs for an 1800 estate. The result was a pair of proposals, the Beach Car and the Hunter. The first of these extended the rear of the car and raised the roofline. The distinctive flanks were also toned down so that the panelling was flatter and an estate-style back was incorporated. However, it was felt that the design did not go far enough, as at that time Volvo wanted to inject some excitement into its range, so something more adventurous was called for. This led to the design of the Hunter, which was similar to the Beach Car but which featured a roof which sloped sharply downwards at the rear. The side windows were small and the bodywork looked quite awkward as a result, but the project showed promise because much of the original car could be retained to keep production costs down. Although the Hunter progressed through the clay model and even the prototype stages, the project was canned because it was felt that this still wasn't the car that Volvo wanted at that time.

The next stage was the production of a third prototype, named the Rocket which used elements of both designs. Its barrel-shaped rear end was a huge break from Volvo's usual conservative designs, and it was these graceless lines which led to it being referred to as the 'Barrel'. With much tougher US safety legislation pending, Volvo incorporated a substantial flush-fitting rubber insert for the rear end

Rocket and Viking concepts

Volvo designer Jan Wilsgaard had been working on an estate version of the P1800 since the mid-1960s and the Italian styling house Fissore had also designed and built a prototype fastback 1800 in 1965, so experimentation with the 1800's bodywork was nothing new.

Meanwhile Italy's Carozzeria Coggiola had been briefed to produce a prototype sports estate based on the 1800. The result was the 1800ES, but Coggiola did not stop there. With the 1800 being so long in the tooth in 1971, the styling house was also commissioned to come up with a replacement for the 1800 coupé.

The outcome was the Viking, presented at the 1971 Paris Salon. Also known as the 1800ESC, the rakish hatchback used the mechanicals of the 1800ES and it was well-received by press and public alike. When *Road & Track* wrote about the concept they declared that this was 'a logical way for Volvo's sports model to go'.

They also suggested replacing the 2.0-litre four-pot with a compact V6 to improve performance and take it a bit further upmarket, but it wasn't to be, as Volvo abandoned the sports market less than two years later.

This was the car that could have replaced the 1800 coupé. Styled by Coggiola, the Viking was fitted with a 2.0-litre engine, but a bigger powerplant could easily have been fitted.

The Rocket was also nicknamed the 'Barrel', and although the car's front panels weren't changed much, it was all new behind the B-pillar – and it was far too radical for Volvo to put into production.

The Saint and the P1800

When Leslie Charteris wrote his first book featuring Simon Templar – alias The Saint – in 1930, his wheels of choice was a Hirondel. But when it came to creating a series for the small screen in the 1960s, Hirondels were rather hard to find (the marque in fact being mythical), so a Jaguar E-type was chosen instead. Perhaps surprisingly, Jaguar could not provide an E-type or any mock-up interiors at short notice for Simon Templar to drive, so an alternative had to be found. At that stage nobody knew whether or not the programme would be a success, but unfortunately for Jaguar, it was a big hit.

The alternative was a car which Roger Moore, the programme's star, came across quite by chance – a white Volvo P1800. In the absence of the first choice from Jaguar, Volvo was asked to supply a P1800 to be used in The Saint and within a week of the request 71 DXC had been delivered to the programme's producers, Associated Television. No discounts were available on either the car or the mock-up interiors which were produced specially for the programme and the following year a second car was supplied, and which must rate as one of the most successful examples of product placement ever. Carrying the

registration 77 GYL, the second car is now displayed in the Cars of the Stars Museum in Keswick, Cumbria.

Although the Volvo was replaced by a Jaguar XJ-S in some of the 1970s editions of the series, when a feature film of The Saint was made in 1997, it was to Volvo that the producer turned. Although an XK8 could have been used to maintain a Jaguar theme, a C70 was opted for to continue the association with Volvo.

Perhaps one of the most enduring screen pairings ever, Simon Templar and his white 1800 featured in more than 100 episodes of The Saint TV series.

and the rear wings were blended into the upper panelling. In the end, it was felt that not only would the tooling costs be prohibitively high but Volvo's traditional customers would be frightened off by such a radical shape.

Ultimately, the production car was styled in-house by the company's chief designer Jan Wilsgaard. He opted for a two-plus-two configuration which, in reality, was a comfortable two-seater with plenty of carrying space – especially with the rear seats folded down.

When the car went on sale in 1971 it cost £2,650, for which you could have had a sports estate from the stables of Reliant or BMW. When *Car* magazine pitched the 1800ES against the Scimitar GTE and BMW 2000 Touring it was clear that the Volvo trailed well behind the offerings from Tamworth and Munich from a performance point of view. At a few pennies under £3,000, the Swedish product was also over £600 more expensive than the other two – and it wasn't as though equipment levels were much higher, although disc brakes all round and overdrive fitted as standard were something the others could not claim. The magazine's testers were unequivocal in their summary: when it came to dynamics the 1800 was well behind its competitors.

At least *Car & Driver* gave the 1800ES a more favourable review – probably because the car was tested in isolation rather than against its competitors. In any case, the Scimitar, which offered an extra pair of cylinders, was not available in North America. The publication's testers reckoned that jettisoning the coupé bodystyle in favour of an estate was just what was needed – the car was now much more usable without sacrificing anything. Noise levels were still too high (a verdict which *The Autocar* agreed with wholeheartedly), but it was still a relaxing tourer – and after all, Volvo was selling it as a long-distance cruiser rather than an uncom-promising sports car.

Series identification

The prototype 1800 was known as the P958 and once in production each model year of the 1800 was identified by a series letter – although all the Jensen-built cars are known as Series A models. The first Swedish-made examples from 1963 carry the Series B tag while those constructed the following year are known as Series D versions – for some reason there was no Series C.

A bit more predictably, the 1965 1800s were known as Series E cars, with Series F following in 1966. Somebody must have forgotten where the system had got up to by 1967 because Series M was chosen to identify these cars, while 1969 examples carry the Series S tag.

The Series T 1800 arrived in 1970, complete with Bosch Jetronic fuel injection and the following year saw the appearance of the Series U cars. The final year of 1800 assembly (1971) saw the introduction of the Series W 1800E and when the coupé was dropped in favour of the 1800ES, the first of the estates were also Series W models. With production of the 1800ES lasting such a short time, it was no surprise that the last of the line were the Series Y, built during 1972–1973.

Time was finally called on the 1800 in June 1973, when the 1800ES went out of production. US safety regulations meant the car would have had to be re-engineered with 5mph (8kph) impact bumpers from the 1974 model year onwards, and the sums just did not add up. It was ironic that the 1800's largest market was also the one which killed it off. The USA had taken more than three-quarters of Volvo's production, with the second-largest market, the UK, taking just over 1,000 examples. Within another couple of decades however, Volvo would return to the compact sports estate market, with its first front-wheel drive production car, the 480ES.

Driving the P1800

The P1800 is no featherweight, with more than 22cwt (1,118kg) to pull along, so performance isn't electrifying. But once up to speed it cruises along quite happily at 80mph (129kph) without fuss – this is a car for cruising rather than enjoying twisty B-roads. The engine's humble origins are hard to disguise, and its lack of sophistication is evident as you accelerate through the gears, but it is far from unpleasant.

The seats in the coupé versions of the 1800 are not very supportive but move over to an 1800ES and you will find the comfort on offer a revelation. The extra headroom allowed Volvo to redesign the seats so they became far more comfortable to use. Despite a lack of power assistance the steering isn't unduly heavy – the thin-rimmed steering wheel makes things a lot easier thanks to its generous diameter. Whichever version of the 1800 you're piloting, the ride and handling are perfectly good, if not the best available.

Whichever 1800 you try you will find it gets hot inside, a situation which isn't helped by the car having such an effective heater. You need to make sure it is completely switched off or it will quickly get like a sauna in there!

Irv Gordon's 2 million-mile 1800S

When he was 25 years old, in 1966, Irv Gordon bought a new 1800S from his local Volvo dealer, having fallen in love with the car after seeing it in *The Saint* TV series. A visit to Volvoville and he was hooked – the fins and the cherry red paint were just what he was after.

Having paid $4,150 for the car, it would be hard to argue that he hadn't got value for money as by the end of the weekend that he purchased the car he had already clocked up 1,500 miles. By 1999 he'd covered 1,675,000 miles (2,695,000km) – enough to earn a place in the *Guinness Book of Records* for the car with the most miles under its belt. By the spring of 2002 he'd cracked the two million-mile mark and still the car is going strong.

Along the way there have been around 660 oil changes – Gordon

insists that the oil is changed every 3,000 miles (4,800km) and that is why the engine has been rebuilt just once so far, after 680,000 miles (1,940,000km).

The car has never broken down and the only time it didn't manage to get to its destination under its own steam was when a tractor trailer was driven into the front of the car, damaging the radiator. As a result of the huge number of miles

In Volvo circles Irv Gordon is something of a legend, having clocked up more than two million miles in his 1800 coupé as well as many in a 780 given to him by Volvo.

so far racked up, Gordon has become something of a celebrity in the USA. When his car reached the one million-mile mark he was given a new Volvo 780 to mark the occasion, and thanks to his high profile in Volvo circles, he has even had a phrase coined after him. Called an 'Irv', the saying denotes a million miles – but there aren't many owners who have clocked up a single 'Irv', never mind two of them.

Buying a P1800

1. Patching up the front end after a shunt isn't very easy, so if the panel alignment – especially the bonnet – is variable or the grille surround looks out of kilter it is probably because at some point somebody has been a bit careless.

2. The front panels are also the first to show signs of rust. The metal around the headlamps and sidelights is especially likely to house rot, along with the areas around the wheelarch lips and the leading edge of the sills.

3. Replacing wings properly is tricky and the inner wings succumb to corrosion all too readily as well. Look inside the wheelarch towards the top of the front wing – if you can see rust it will be found to be a lot worse once the wing is removed.

4. The sills are also likely to be rotten, and if the genuine Volvo panels haven't been used the correct curved profile won't be there. Also missing will be the vertical grooves below the door, but they could also not be there because the sills are full of filler, so be very wary.

5. From underneath, check the front crossmember (underneath the radiator): it has four sides, any of which can rot, and it is a nightmare to replace because it's welded all round. While you're under the car also inspect the front outriggers along with the steering box mountings. In the case of the former, genuine Volvo panels are the best ones to go for. Other common rot spots include the fuel filler area, the bottom of the doors, the floorpans and the bootlid.

6. Because only a partial rubber seal was fitted along the top of the door, the casings fill up with water. As a result, if the drain holes are allowed to block, the lower edge of the door will corrode. Gutters don't rot too badly, except on ES models which are more vulnerable for some reason.

7. The bonnet hinges can seize up, and because they're mounted on a notably thin mounting panel, the panel bends and breaks if the hinges aren't lubricated properly.

8. Engine maladies are the same as for the Amazon and gearboxes are amazingly durable, but if run with insufficient oil, the bearings will become worn and you will find it gets increasingly noisy. The sign that gives it away is that top gear is quieter than all the others.

9. The steering shouldn't be at all heavy. If it seems as though something isn't quite right, it is probably because the steering box has been overtightened. This will lead to premature wear of the box so it is best to make sure the unit is set up properly if you want to avoid large bills later on.

10. Getting original interior trim for the P1800 is now pretty much impossible, although all examples had leather-trimmed seats, so getting those recovered isn't difficult. If it is just a question of the seat having collapsed, you can fit new webbing yourself very cheaply to restore their shape.

11. Although the braking system is normally reliable, a lack of use will lead to it seizing up. Even then, it is not the end of the world, but you will need a special hub puller for the rear brakes on pre-1968 cars.

Despite Volvo's reputation for stodgy driving characteristics, the 1800 is actually very good dynamically, and an excellent classic buy for regular use.

The 140 and 160 *series*

The Amazon continued to be sold alongside the 144 for a couple of years, but the arrival of Volvo's all-new saloon heralded a new look that would last nearly three decades.

U ntil the mid-1960s, Volvo had a reputation for cars which were good to drive (although not necessarily a dynamic delight), and were distinctive in appearance. Then the 140 series arrived and it was all downhill from there. In short, the 140 and all the series which followed were styling disasters, even if the cars did have their devotees. Safe and durable they may have been, but many people were put off driving something that looked like a tank, although those who did buy a Volvo were often drawn to them because of the anti-style statement they were

140 series
1966–1974

ENGINE:
Four cylinders in line, iron block and head
Bore x stroke   84m x 80mm
Capacity   1,778cc
Valvegear: Overhead valve
Compression ratio: 10.0:1
Fuelling: Twin SU HS6
Maximum power: 85bhp (SAE) at 5,000rpm
Maximum torque: 109lb ft at 3,000rpm

TRANSMISSION:
Rear-wheel-drive; Four-speed all-synchro
Final drive ratio: 4.1:1 (without overdrive)
                       4.56:1 (with overdrive)

SUSPENSION:
Front: Independent with coil springs, telescopic
dampers, wishbones, anti-roll bar
Rear: Live axle, upper and lower radius arms,
Panhard rod, anti-roll bar

STEERING:
Type   Cam and roller
Turns lock-to-lock   4.1

BRAKES:
Front & Rear: Disc
Servo assistance standard

WHEELS/TYRES:
5in pressed steel wheels with 165 x 15in
tyres

BODYWORK:
All-steel monocoque
Two-door saloon, four-door saloon, five-door
estate

DIMENSIONS:
Length   15ft 3in (4.64m)
Wheelbase   8ft 6in (2.59m)
Track   4ft 5in (1.34m)
Width   5ft 8in (1.72m)
Height   4ft 9in (1.45m)

WEIGHT: 2,800–2,889lb
                       (1,270–1,300kg)

PERFORMANCE: (Source: *Motor*)
Max speed   102mph
0–60mph   12.5sec
30–50mph in top   9.8sec (17.7 sec
                       overdrive top)
50–70mph in top   10.9sec (18.8sec
                       overdrive top)

UK PRICE WHEN NEW (May 1967):
Four-door saloon   £1,415
                       (£1,489 with overdrive)

NUMBER MADE:
142   412,986
144   523,808
145   268,317

164
1968–1975

ENGINE:
Six cylinders in line, cast-iron block and head
Bore x stroke   88.9mm x 80mm
Capacity: 2,978cc
Valvegear: Overhead valve
Compression ratio: 9.3:1
Fuelling: two Zenith-Stromberg
                       carburettors
Maximum power: 145bhp (SAE) at 5,500rpm
Maximum torque: 163lb ft at 3,000rpm

TRANSMISSION:
Rear-wheel drive
Four-speed all-synchro manual or three-speed
auto
Final drive ratio: 3.73:1
                       3.31:1 optional

SUSPENSION:
Front: Independent with coil springs, telescopic
dampers, wishbones, anti-roll bar
Rear: Live axle, coil springs, telescopic dampers,
transverse link, twin trailing radius arms

STEERING:
Type: Recirculating ball
Turns lock-to-lock: 4.8 (3.7 turns lock-to-
                       lock on PAS cars)

BRAKES:
Front & Rear: Disc
Servo assistance standard

WHEELS/TYRES:
4.5 x 15in wheels with 165 SR15 tyres

BODYWORK:
All-steel monocoque, four-door saloon
DIMENSIONS:
Length   15ft 5in (4.7m)
Wheelbase   8ft 10in (2.69m)
Track   4ft 5in (1.34m)
Width   5ft 8in (1.72m)
Height   4ft 9in (1.45m)

WEIGHT: 2,990lb (1,357kg)

PERFORMANCE: (Source: *Autocar*)
Max speed   107mph
0–60mph   12.8sec
30–50mph in second 6.9sec
50–70mph in second 8.3sec

UK PRICE WHEN NEW (April 1970)
Four-door saloon £2,211

NUMBER MADE:
146,008 (all types)

164E
1972–1975

As 164 except:
ENGINE:
Compression ratio   10:1
Fuelling   Bosch electronic fuel
                       injection
Maximum power   160bhp (DIN) at 5,500rpm
Maximum torque   170lb ft at 2,500rpm

WHEELS/TYRES:
5.5in wheels with 175 x 15in tyres

WEIGHT: 3,192lb (1,450kg)

PERFORMANCE: (Source: *Autocar*)
Max speed   120mph
0–60mph   10.0sec
30–50mph in
overdrive top: 12.2sec
50–70mph
in overdrive top: 14.0sec

UK PRICE WHEN NEW (September 1973):
Two-door saloon: £2,966

making. By the early 1970s Volvo was clearly sensitive to this. The company even went so far as to put together an advert which posed a 144 next to an M-48 tank and then compared the two. Using the heading: 'The execution is different, but the concept is basically the same,' it was good to see that Volvo's advertising agency had a sense of humour! But although the advertising department didn't mind some self-deprecation, when it was inflicted by others the marketing department was rather more sober. When *Car* magazine splashed the 140 series across its front cover in 1972, with the strap line: 'The car as an appliance,' Volvo was not amused. Advertising was pulled from the publication for a decade and the company's cars continued to be the butt of *Car* – and other magazines' – jokes for years to come.

Throughout the 1970s, '80s and well into the '90s, Volvo was in a styling wilderness. To be fair though, when the 140 arrived in 1966 it was modern and the styling was crisp. Few of its competitors were especially stylish and the car's build quality certainly put it above pretty much anything else, but over the next 20 years many of Volvo's competitors moved on to more adventurous styling and the company was gradually left further and further behind.

There was one facet however that put the 140 series ahead of its competitors – the built-in safety features. The PV444 had pioneered a small number of innovations and the Amazon went on to introduce many more. By the time the 140 was in development it was abundantly clear to all at Volvo that this was the perfect opportunity to start the safety bandwagon rolling. The problem was that for many years rival manufacturers had enjoyed the upper hand when it came to advertising and selling cars because safety wasn't something that many buyers put very high on their list of priorities. Image, performance and style were more important, but by

the start of the 1970s just about every manufacturer would be jumping on to the safety bandwagon as safety car concepts were rolled out at one motor show after another.

It was in June 1960 that work had begun on the car which it was hoped would replace the 120 series. The Amazon would be supplying all the mechanicals, and there would be an all-new bodyshell. Despite the car being a clean-sheet design, Jan Wilsgaard, who had been briefed with styling the car, would have to retain the Amazon's 102.4in (2.6m) wheelbase. He was also told how wide the track would have to be along with the front and rear windscreen angles and that initially, he would have to come up with two-door and four-door saloons as well as a five-door estate. This did not bode well for design freedom.

As was customary for Volvo at the time, external designers were asked to come up with styling proposals. In this case it was Ghia and Frua, who submitted their ideas in May 1962, but by the time these designs were handed in, the basic bodyshell design had already been decided. So, unless they came up with something pretty special, there was no possibility of their designs even being considered. Sure enough, in the end it was Wilsgaard's design which was chosen, the final styling themes having been laid down in 1961.

From the outset, the intention with the new car was to increase production capacity massively, and hence global sales. There was plenty of room to increase the size of the Torslanda factory, but the whole project was something of a gamble. Until the car's launch in 1966, the Amazon was the most expensive Volvo saloon, with the PV544 below it. The 140 would slot in above the Amazon, which would remain in production, while the PV544 would no longer be built. In other words, Volvo was going upmarket – but would such a strategy be successful? Although the new car would

Like the Duett and Amazon estate before it, the estate version of the 140 series – the 145 – was extremely popular with those who wanted space and durability.

eventually replace the Amazon, initially, the two models were sold side by side.

The 140 was 7½in (19cm) longer and 4in (10cm) wider than the Amazon whose mechanicals it borrowed and although the wheelbase of both cars was the same at 102.4in, there was much more interior space in the 140. When *Cars & Car Conversions* tested a 144 in October 1966 they were not especially impressed with any particular aspect of the car except one – its safety credentials. Rivals such as the Triumph 2000, Ford Zephyr and Vauxhall's Cresta could match the 144 for comfort, driver appeal and equipment levels, but when it came to safety none of them could even come close. In fact, the magazine's writer went on to say that with the exception of Rolls-Royce, nobody had gone beyond the safety levels built into the 144's braking system. For the first time ever, Volvo had fitted disc brakes all round to one of its cars – and mixed with that was a diagonally split hydraulic system which allowed substantial braking power to be retained (albeit at a reduced level) if one of the circuits failed.

But of course, the safety features did not end there – a laminated windscreen was fitted, which popped out if hit hard enough. There was also a collapsible steering column, rear seatbelt mountings and stronger doorlocks to prevent the doors flying open in an impact. Headrests to reduce whiplash injuries were also standard as was a remarkably stiff monocoque with crumple zones that could withstand amazingly severe impacts.

Pehr Gyllenhammar

When Pehr Gustaf Gyllenhammar joined Volvo in 1971 as CEO and president of the group, there were many who were very concerned about his appointment. At just 36 years of age there were doubts about his ability, while the fact that he was the son-in-law of Gunnar Engellau – the man he was succeeding – did not go down very well.

A lawyer who had studied management, he had already headed the giant Swedish insurance giant Skandia. When he took his new position at Volvo he was well aware of the company's success, and was clear from the outset that complacency was a major problem in such companies. To ensure that neither he nor his company became too comfortable with their success

he invited ordinary employees to join the board, allowing them to have their say in the running of the company – something which subsequently became law in Sweden.

Throughout his 22 years as head of Volvo, Gyllenhammar struck many deals, some of which were more successful than others. His first big deal was the acquisition of Daf, which reached fruition in 1972. Although this did not seem a very shrewd move at first, with the 343 proving to be a disaster, things looked up once the problems of poor build quality had been addressed. A proposed merger with Saab came to nothing, but an alliance with Renault came close to fruition and was the cause of Gyllenhammar's downfall.

Renault and Volvo had already

collaborated on the PRV V6 engine, along with Peugeot, but in January 1990, the announcement was made that Volvo and Renault were to collaborate on various projects to allow them both to develop cars more cheaply. Gyllenhammar relinquished his roles as president and CEO to Christer Zetterberg soon after, so that he could concentrate on facilitating the tie-up. Then, in September 1993, a declaration was made that Volvo and Renault would be merging – but he had not counted on the staff at Volvo who were set against such a move, and the media were soon calling for Gyllenhammar's blood. By December, he had resigned, taking the whole board with him.

The interior styling of the 140 series, like the exterior, was safe in its design, but more importantly, it kept the occupants as safe as possible in the event of an accident.

Suspension was a development of the system used on the Amazon estate, but for the 144 the rear axle was supported by coil springs and telescopic dampers while there were twin radius arms, a Panhard rod, and an anti-roll bar. The result was superb, with the press generally surprised at the car's good handling.

At launch there was a choice of two cars, both four-door saloons but with different states of tune. They were both powered by Volvo's tried-and-tested B18 powerplant, offering 85bhp in the single-carb standard car

and 100bhp in the 144S, thanks to twin SU carburettors. Buyers of the S model could choose between standard or overdrive manual gearboxes, while those who opted for either car could specify an automatic gearbox if required.

In September 1967, a two-door saloon, the 142, arrived and six months later, the five-door estate was introduced, badged as the 145. It was only the bodystyles which differed between the cars – under the skin they were all mechanically identical. The 142 was especially unsuccessful as buyers could not understand why a large four-seater saloon should have just a pair of doors. By 1969, Volvo realised that UK buyers did not want the car, so it was phased out here, although it continued in production for other markets. The 144 and 145 were much more popular, and in 1968, the 1,986cc engine was fitted to all cars in the 140 range, endowing them with more sprightly performance. This was the B20 unit and in single-carburettor form it put out 90bhp, but buyers who opted for the twin-carb version had 118bhp to play with – a useful improvement over

the previous 100bhp.

Exports continued to grow, with over 33,000 cars being sold in America in 1967 and the following year the 140 series became Sweden's best-selling car. This was partly facilitated by Sweden's taxi drivers moving over to 144s, thanks to Volvo building a derivative of the car especially for them. Designated the 144 Taxi and launched in Spring 1968, the 145-based car featured stronger suspension, a glass partition behind the driver, an automatic gearbox and easily cleaned rear seat trim. Available in black or white, the car was just what Sweden's taxi drivers needed, as the Amazon was too cramped for them and the earlier taxis produced by the company were long obsolete.

America was gearing up to impose a lot of new safety legislation for 1969, and although in the 140 series, Volvo had a car which needed virtually no modifications to meet these laws, money was spent making the cars even safer. As a result, changes for the 1970 model year were slight, but there was a new addition to the family in the form of the 145 Express. Loosely intended to replace the now-obsolete Duett/210, the new car was a 145 with a raised roof to allow more room for carrying large loads. From the following year, a van version was available without side windows.

In August 1970, came the next major change, which was the option of fuel injection. In typical Volvo fashion there was no shouting from the rooftops, with just a GL badge denoting that Bosch electronic petrol injection was under the bonnet in place of the carburettors still fitted to cars which carried the De Luxe tag. For most markets the B20B engine was superseded by the slightly uprated B20D unit, which now offered 105bhp (SAE) and had a flatter

torque curve to make the car more enjoyable to drive. Topping the range was the new 142GL, which was a two-door version of the 140 powered by the fuel-injected B20E engine in 130bhp (SAE) form. For those who wanted less equipment but all the power and refinement of the B20E powerplant, there was also the option of the 142E, which went down a storm with *Road & Track* when they tested one in March 1971: they claimed the 142E was 'the best 142 yet'.

It was around this time that Volvo celebrated the production of its two-millionth car. A yellow 144, the car was donated to the Red Cross for use in Switzerland. But soon after, it became apparent that a different

The four-door 144 won no prizes for beauty, but its styling was crisp and up to date when it was launched in 1966.

Left: The two-door saloon version of the 140 series – the 142 – didn't sell especially well outside Sweden, but in the home market it was often more popular than the four-door car.

Right: These water-damaged 144s were going to be scrapped until somebody suggested they should be used to demonstrate the strength of the car's bodyshell.

yellow 144, also claimed to be the two-millionth Volvo built, had been donated to a British charity for use in the UK. (Nobody has yet claimed to know of a third two-millionth car, but somewhere in North America there's probably one lurking . . .)

In the spring of 1972 came a huge leap forward for Volvo, with the opening of its Volvo Technical Centre. After the construction of its Torslanda factory, this represented the biggest single investment for Volvo because it allowed in-house development for just about every aspect of Volvo's cars. As well as laboratories that enabled testing to be performed on materials and emissions, there were also a wind tunnel and a climate chamber. Not only that, but a safety centre meant crash testing could be performed to simulate most types of collision under controlled conditions.

In 1972, a revised 140 series made its debut, although changes were definitely evolutionary rather than revolutionary. A narrower grille with different headlamps and indicators replaced the previous full-width affair, and there was an all-new dash in place of the previous slabby effort. It was clear by this stage that the 140 series was showing its age, and minor changes were no longer enough to hide the car's faults. When *Motor* tested a 144 in March 1973 they commended the car on its good

As a premium car, neither a two-door nor an estate version of the 164 were deemed appropriate. That view changed considerably just over a decade later, when large Volvo estate cars became especially popular.

If Volvo was to compete with established European prestige marques such as Mercedes, a six-cylinder engine had to be offered. By adding two cylinders, the 140 series became the 160 series, or more specifically the 164 as this was the only car in the series. It certainly got the approval of the workforce.

heating and ventilation along with its numerous standard safety features, but a harsh, noisy engine did it no favours and neither did its poor roadholding in the wet, its woolly steering or its firm ride. It was no better when *Autocar* tested a 144DL later that year, with just the same verdict being reached – the car was undeniably very solidly built, but it was so mediocre dynamically, that mere durability was no longer enough. In the seven years since the car had been introduced a lot of new competitors had come along and Volvo's executive saloons were now starting to look very dated – even if none of its rivals could match it in terms of safety.

The final version of the 140 series was shown just a year after the MkII was first seen. Because 5mph (8kph) bumpers were now

compulsory in the USA, Volvo found it easier to produce all its cars with them, regardless of which market they would be sold in – after all, America took most of the cars that Volvo exported. In countries outside the USA the bumpers did not have the hydraulic rams that were fitted to US-spec cars to make them true 5mph bumpers, but they still kept the ungainly looks. Yet despite the less-than-glowing reviews which the 140 was receiving by the time it ceased production in 1974, in the last full year of production, which was 1973, no fewer than 218,155 examples were built and sold. The 140 series might have fallen somewhat out of favour with many reviewers, but for those who were having to put their own money into a car, it seemed that the 140 still held much appeal.

Marcos-Volvo 3-litre

The first Marcos fitted with a Volvo engine was the B18-engined 1800 launched at the 1964 Racing Car Show. Mildly tuned to give 114bhp at 5,800rpm in standard form, this powerplant could be tuned further if needed and was wonderfully reliable while offering ideal weight, size and torque characteristics. It was also expensive, so in 1966, the Volvo unit was dropped in favour of the 1,499cc engine fitted to the Mk1 Ford Cortina GT.

Until the end of the 1960s it would be Ford engines that were generally fitted to the Marcos, all sorts of options being offered including different engines and tuning packages, but when

Marcos found that Ford's European engines could not meet impending US emissions regulations it was back to Volvo that the company turned, this time choosing the 164's 2,978cc powerplant for a new 3-litre model introduced in 1971.

Generating 145bhp at 5,500rpm, the Volvo engine was significantly more powerful than the Ford V6 Marcos also offered and with a four-speed gearbox without overdrive the car was capable of 125mph (200kph).

The 0–60mph sprint could also be despatched in little more than seven seconds and because the unit could be tuned so easily, the Marcos could be turned into a

seriously quick car without any difficulty at all.

Because of the twin carburettors fitted to the 164 engine there were clearance problems which necessitated amendments to the car's bonnet which made it look a bit unbalanced, but apart from that, the Volvo engine was ideal. In 1972, Marcos went bust after 27 cars fitted with these Volvo engines had been impounded in the US towards the end of the previous year. The company already had cashflow problems and US Customs, refusing to release the cars for several weeks while they deliberated on whether or not the cars could legally be sold, was the final straw.

The front section of the 164 was significantly longer than that of the 140 series, to accommodate the in-line six-cylinder powerplant.

The 164

Considering Volvo had built its name on six-cylinder cars during the pre-war years, such models were notable by their absence from the company's range after the Second World War. In August 1968 this was remedied with the announcement of the 164, effectively a six-cylinder version of the 144. But it wasn't quite as simple as that, as the 164 had an extended wheelbase to allow for an engine bay long enough to house the longer engine block.

Work had started on the car as far back as March 1958, when the 800 series had gone out of production. Volvo could no longer supply limousine-style cars for taxi or VIP use so a project began to create a new large car. A V8 engine was envisaged initially, but by May 1960 it was clear that a six-cylinder powerplant would be more appropriate. At that stage it was reckoned that production would begin towards the middle of the decade but a survey carried out in 1960 showed that large cars were falling out of favour. Volvo wasn't prepared to risk building a larger car only for buyers to shun it and as a result the project was canned.

However, with good progress being made on development of the 140 series by 1962, it became apparent that the new car could be used as a basis for a larger car that was only new from the A-pillars forward. So, although the 164 was very much like its four-cylinder sibling from the A-pillars back, it was conceived as a much more exclusive car with an increased amount of standard equipment and a more ostentatious front end. This allowed Volvo to retain buyers who had otherwise decided to trade up from a Volvo to a Mercedes, as they had been unable to find anything in the Swedish company's range which suited their needs. In Britain especially, the Volvo option was welcome for thousands of buyers who had lost interest in cars from Ford, Vauxhall and BMC. These were the people who were fed up with poor British quality and wanted something better – something which the Volvo could provide.

The interior space of the 164 was the same as the 144's, but the 2,978cc B30 straight-six gave the car performance that was far ahead of its smaller brother. This engine was essentially a 144 engine increased in size by 50 per cent – many of the internals were shared and with its seven-bearing crankshaft the cylinder block was really just a B20 engine with a pair of cylinders added. Twin Zenith-Stromberg carburettors were fitted to give 145bhp at 5,500rpm and either manual/overdrive or automatic gearboxes could be fitted.

P172 coupé prototype

Intended as a replacement for the 1800S in the late 1960s, the P172 (initially known as the 16S) took the concept of a sporty Volvo upmarket. The plan was to base the car on the floorpan and running gear of the six-cylinder 164 saloon, which was due for launch in 1968. That would have meant a 3-litre six-cylinder engine to give the car decent performance, and whereas the 2,978cc powerplant developed 135bhp in the 164, the aim was to tune it to produce 180bhp in the P172. With a cast-iron construction for both the block and the head, it needed all the power it could get.

The car would be significantly larger than the 1800, the aim being to produce a grand tourer for covering long distances with great ease. Once again it was the American market that was the focus for the car, and at a projected $6,000, it would be eminently affordable. There would be just a two-door fixed-head coupé, using standard 164 suspension. To keep weight down, extensive use of aluminium was originally considered, but as the project matured it was decided that steel would be the most cost-effective option. The triple-carburettor set-up that was initially envisaged was also dispensed with in favour of fuel injection, after it became clear that keeping such a fuelling system in tune would potentially be a nightmare for Volvo's dealer network.

The P172 was intended to be a lavish luxury car, with room for four adults to tour in comfort. Although manual transmission was standard, there would be the choice of an automatic gearbox along with power steering and right-hand drive. The P172 was even designed with modification to a convertible in mind, as Volvo was all too aware of the difficulty of turning the 1800 into a drophead, which it would dearly liked to have done.

The US dealer network reckoned there would not be enough demand for the car to warrant full-scale production. Investment in tooling for the new bodyshell would have been high and there wasn't the production capacity at the Torslanda plant to build it anyway. So in the end, the project was aborted, before a running prototype had even been built.

Zagato GTZ prototypes

Italian coachbuilder Zagato first turned its attentions to rebodying a Volvo for the 1969 Turin Motor Show. Based on a 144 floorpan, and with the mechanicals completely unchanged, the GTZ was the first rebodying of a Volvo just for display at a motor show.

Zagato had no intention of putting the car into production – the concept was merely a way of garnering publicity for the company. Although the GTZ was fairly quickly forgotten, that did not stop Zagato from producing a second Volvo-based concept. This time it was named the 3000GTZ and was built for the 1971 Geneva Motor Show. Again, the underpinnings were unchanged, but instead of a 144 it was the 164 whose floorpan was used. Whereas the earlier car's lines were uncontroversial, the later car was pretty ungainly with odd proportions and a Volvo grille sitting between pop-up headlamps – a combination which did not work at all.

The 164-based Zagato GTZ did not look great from the rear – but it was even worse from the front! This proposal was soon forgotten after being shown at the 1971 Geneva Motor Show.

Being the flagship of the range, the 164 was well equipped, although leather trim was not standard until the autumn of 1969. Most cars sold in export markets were equipped with electrically operated sunroof and windows along with air-conditioning, a stereo and tinted glass. By the autumn of 1970 power steering had become standard on all 164s and a year later there was the option of a fuel-injected version with the announcement of the 164E. Using Bosch electronic fuel injection, this new car was significantly more powerful than the carb-fed car, offering 175bhp instead of 145bhp – enough to give the car a genuine 120mph (193kph) top speed.

Even without fuel injection the 164 was a true executive express. *Autosport* tested one in December 1969 and claimed that the 'new Volvo 164 is in the chauffeur-driven class, but with the kind of performance to attract the master to the wheel'. The test car was fitted with the optional 3.73:1 rear axle ratio which made its performance even more impressive than the standard model with its 3.31:1 differential. Although it made the car somewhat busier once it had got going, the low-down performance was nothing short of astonishing, with the 0–60mph sprint being despatched in just over 10 seconds. When *Autocar* tested a 164E in September 1973, fuel injection had become standard on all 164s, the carburettor-equipped cars having been dropped that summer. The magazine's road testers were more equivocal about the 164's capabilities, reckoning that there were as many points in favour of buying one as there were against. High purchase and running costs were tempered by good safety levels and excellent high-speed refinement – but it was no driver's car, thanks to its heavy brakes and vague steering.

At the same time as the arrival of the fuel-injected engine, the dashboard was revised and ventilated brake discs fitted but just

Buying the 140 and 160 series

1. Although engines are long-lived, they can get noisy when the camshafts wear. Your patience will wear out before the camshaft does though, and replacement is easy. The fibre timing gear also wears, and replacing with steel is a good idea although these aren't as quiet. If the engine is running erratically it is probably because the carburettors are out of balance. Be especially wary of Strombergs, which are not as easy to balance as the SUs.

2. The rear oil seal on the gearbox tends to leak, allowing the unit to drain gradually. The transmission will end up irreparably damaged if the oil level is allowed to drop too far. If the car does need a new gearbox (or even if it doesn't) it's worth fitting an overdrive unit if there isn't one fitted already.

3. Rot is now a problem on these cars, with sills and wheelarches especially vulnerable. The front wings bolt on, which means changing them is easy when they corrode, as they tend to. Four-cylinder cars received different wings after September 1972 – earlier cars can be modified to accept later-style wings, but doing things the other way round is tricky.

a year later there were more significant changes to coincide with a facelifted 140 series. This meant heavier bumpers, modified rear lights, reinforced doors and a shortened grille – while 1975 model year cars, which were the last ones, had no quarterlights. The last 164 was built in 1975, by which time 146,008 had rolled off the production lines. The car had proved a major export success for Volvo and the launch of the six-cylinder 260 series later that year showed the company had no intention of abandoning the luxury saloon market.

Driving the 140 and 160 series

Although the 144 is no sports car, it is far better to drive than it is to look at. There is a feeling of solidity that is very reassuring and excellent brakes

(discs all round) pull you up from high speed without any fuss.

There is not too much road noise and wind noise is reasonably well muted, although the car's bluff lines don't help very much here. What is perhaps the most disappointing aspect of the car's performance is the engine noise, as it can get quite intrusive under acceleration.

The seating position is very comfortable, but the seats don't support you that well when you get enthusiastic behind the wheel. The gearshift is smooth and all the controls are light – the car might have a reputation for being heavy, but it is certainly not heavy to drive.

The 164 is much the same as its smaller brother, but even better to drive, the increased power making it more accelerative, more relaxing, and smoother. The power-assisted steering is a bit overlight when up to speed, but it is really quite fun to pilot.

The 240 and 260 series

By the time the 244 replaced the 144, Volvo had a well-established reputation for boxy cars that put safety, reliability and practicality before anything else. The 244 perpetuated that philosophy and was incredibly successful.

Production of the 140 series ended in 1974 with the last 164 coming off the line the following year. These models were replaced by the 240 series and the 264 respectively, with the introduction of the latter paving the way for a whole new range of six-cylinder cars. Looking like a cross between the 140/160 series and the VESC (see Chapter 7), the 200 series was immediately identifiable as a Volvo – square, slabby lines and the appearance of great weight with little in the way of grace. But it seemed that buyers didn't especially care, because this was a car which built on the selling points of Volvo's earlier cars – safety, comfort and reliability. Generous crumple zones now replaced the particularly ungainly bumpers that had been fitted to the last of the 140/160 series. Although the B20 engine which had been fitted to earlier Volvos was still available, there was a new engine on offer in the 240, in the shape of the B21 overhead cam unit, an engine that was able to meet the increasingly tough emissions standards set by the North American market. Perhaps more importantly, there was a whole range of cars available from the outset because two, four and five-door versions of the 140 series had been developed, and the 240 was merely a development of the 140 rather than an all-new model.

Indeed, aft of the A-pillars there were relatively few changes although from the windscreen forward most of the metalwork was new, so that MacPherson struts could be adopted along with more progressive crumple zones to make the car safer in the event of a collision. Rack-and-pinion steering also made an appearance, and was much sharper than the cam-and-roller set-up with which the 140 had been equipped. The front and rear ends were now wrapped in thick black rubber-faced bumpers, so that

240 series

1974–1985

ENGINE:
Four cylinders in line, iron block and head
Bore x stroke	92mm x 80mm
Capacity	2,127cc
Valvegear	Overhead valve
Compression ratio	9.3:1
Fuelling	Bosch fuel injection
Maximum power	123bhp (DIN) at 5,500rpm
Maximum torque	130lb ft at 3,500rpm

TRANSMISSION:
Rear-wheel-drive
Four-speed with overdrive
Final drive ratio	4.1:1

SUSPENSION:
Front: Independent with coil springs, MacPherson struts, telescopic dampers, anti-roll bar
Rear: Live axle, coil springs, trailing arms, telescopic dampers, Panhard rod, anti-roll bar

STEERING:
Rack-and-pinion
Turns lock-to-lock	4.3

(Power assistance optional with 2,127cc engine)

BRAKES:
Front & Rear:	Disc

Servo assistance standard

WHEELS/TYRES:
5.5in pressed-steel wheels with 185 x 70–14in tyres

BODYWORK:
All-steel monocoque
Two-door saloon, four-door saloon, five-door estate

DIMENSIONS:
Length	16ft 0in (4.88m)
Wheelbase	8ft 8in (2.64m)
Track	4ft 5in (1.35m)
Width	5ft 7in (1.7m)
Height	4ft 8½in (1.44m)

WEIGHT:	2,950lb (1,338kg)

PERFORMANCE: (Source: Autocar)
Max speed	106mph
0–60mph	11.4sec
30–50mph in overdrive top	14.2sec
50–70mph in overdrive top	14.9sec

UK PRICE WHEN NEW (April 1975):
244 GL	£3,603

NUMBER MADE:
Total	2,685,171
242	242,621
244	1,483,399
245	959,151

240 diesel

As for 240 except:
ENGINE:
Six cylinders in line, iron block and alloy head
Bore x stroke	76.5mm x 86.4mm
Capacity	2,383cc
Valvegear	Overhead camshaft
Compression ratio	23.5:1
Fuelling	Bosch VE injection
Maximum power	82bhp (DIN) at 4,800rpm
Maximum torque	104lb ft at 2,800rpm

TRANSMISSION:
Four-speed with overdrive
Final drive ratio:	3.73:1

WEIGHT:	2,999lb (1,360kg)

PERFORMANCE: (Source: Road & Track)
Max speed	92mph
0–60mph	18.5sec

US PRICE WHEN NEW (September 1980):
Four-door saloon	$12,225

260 series

1974–1981

As for 240 except:
ENGINE:
Six cylinders in line, alloy block and head
Bore x stroke	88mm x 73mm
Capacity	2,664cc
Valvegear	Overhead camshaft
Compression ratio	8.7:1
Fuelling	Bosch fuel injection
Maximum power	140bhp (DIN) at 6,000rpm
Maximum torque	153lb ft at 3,000rpm

TRANSMISSION:
Rear-wheel-drive
Four-speed all-synchro with overdrive
Final drive ratio:	3.73:1

STEERING:
Rack-and-pinion with standard power assistance
Turns lock-to-lock:	3.5

WEIGHT:	3,200lb (1,456kg)

PERFORMANCE: (Source: Autocar)
Max speed	100mph
0–60mph	13.5sec
30–50mph in overdrive top	13.6sec
50–70mph in overdrive top	16.4sec

UK PRICE WHEN NEW (August 1978):
265 GLE	£7,397

they could comply with tougher US crash regulations and it was these which gave the car such an excessive appearance. Boxy – and to some eyes bland – styling was one thing, but such obtrusive bumpers really defaced the car in the view of many commentators.

Although the B20 engine was still available in the entry-level 240, the principal power unit was the new B21, produced in either carburetted or fuel-injected forms. Displacing 2,127cc, this new powerplant shared much – at least on paper – with the B20 engine which had been fitted to

Volvos for so many years. A cast-iron block and five-bearing crankshaft had been seen on the earlier unit, but the new engine was fitted with an aluminium-alloy cylinder head and a belt-driven overhead camshaft. In carburetted B21A form the engine developed 97bhp (DIN) while if the

B21E unit with fuel injection was specified, power output rose to 123bhp, thanks partly to the adoption of electronic ignition.

The really big news was saved for the 260 however, as for this car there was a completely new engine, which was the 2.7-litre 'Douvrin' 90° V6 unit which resulted from the alliance with Peugeot and Renault. This powerplant, badged the B27, was available with fuel injection or twin carburettors and featured twin chain-driven overhead camshafts. Something that was especially significant about the B27 engine was that it was no longer than Volvo's four-cylinder units, which meant that if a four-cylinder car needed to be uprated to six-cylinder specification, the front of the car – or at least the engine bay – did not have to be completely re-engineered to accept the larger powerplant.

The 264 four-door saloon was Volvo's new range topper while at the bottom of the range was the 242 two-door saloon. In between were the four-door saloon and five-door estate, the 244 and 245 respectively, which would earn Volvo most of its money. The fact that the 245 immediately caught on was just what the company needed – failure now would have spelt the end of the company. The introduction of the 240 and 260 series brought with it one innovation which proved to be an unlikely source of publicity for Volvo, and something which helped enormously to bolster its caring-and-sharing image. This was the adoption of a new type of production process at Volvo's Kalmar plant in which the people who assembled the cars no longer had to repeat the same task over and over *ad infinitum*. Instead a group of workers was assigned to an

The carrying capacity of the 1970s Volvo estates (here a 245) was legendary. Fitting in a balloon may have been pushing it a bit, but it was amazing just how much you could get in.

assembly station on a daily basis, where they would carry out a range of tasks between them. Although they would not try out every job possible in the production of a car, over a period of time they would work through a range of assembly processes so that they remained more stimulated than if they were to focus on the same job day in and day out.

In 1975 the 265 estate version of the 260 series was launched and the 240 series was voted Family Car of the Year by readers of America's biggest-selling car magazine, *Car & Driver*. But despite the undoubted popularity of its cars this wasn't an easy time for Volvo, on account of the acquisition of Daf and the quality problems that brought with it, the fuel crisis in 1974, and a huge, 22 per cent wage increase in Sweden. As well as the introduction of a new baby car (the 66) in 1975, Volvo also decided to expand its luxury car range with the launch of a V6-engined 262. A quite different model from the Bertone 262C, this new car was a cross between the two-door 242 and the V6-engined 264. Available for the

The facelifted 240 series, with its rectangular headlamps in place of the circular units fitted previously, looked far more modern than the earlier car, but it was still very boxy!

North American market only, the 262 was a dismal failure because the product planners had not done their work properly. While trying to inject some glamour into the rest of the range, they had failed to appreciate what buyers of the car were likely to want and had offered just a relatively basic level of trim with the less powerful of the two versions of the PRV engine. Within a year the car was obsolete after just 3,239 had been built, but within two years Bertone would introduce a new 262 coupé – the 262C, which is covered separately.

Keen to build on the popularity of the range, Volvo produced a three-door prototype based on the 240 in 1976. Just the one was built and the following year a six-cylinder car was made, called the 263 – the four-cylinder car wore a 243 badge. They looked much better than either the saloon or estates that were already available because they were much less boxy. This was partly the result of the panels ahead of the windscreen having been subtly reshaped as well as a completely new rear end being grafted on; but it was decided that the proposals had little to offer over the estate cars that were already in the showrooms, so they were canned.

For 1976, Volvo came up with a bright idea called the VSG, or Volvo Service Guarantee, which was offered on all new Volvos sold in Sweden, in addition to the standard 12-month guarantee. The VSG ensured that no owner would have to pay more than SKr300 for any service within the first three years of ownership, as long as no more than 60,000km had been covered in that time. It was essentially a forerunner of the modern fixed-price servicing packages that have become common in recent years and because it allowed owners to budget more easily, the guarantee was to prove very popular. This guarantee was not offered outside Sweden and towards the latter part of the 1970s things began to get very difficult for Volvo.

Japanese cars had started to become very popular in the States and partly as a result of this Volvo saw US sales of its cars slide from 58,400 in 1976 to just 43,700 the following year. The big increase in assembly costs hadn't helped either, with the list prices of Volvo's cars increasing by up to 80 per cent between 1972 and 1977. That put the company's cars in direct competition with the products of Cadillac, a company noted for its luxury and heritage – selling points which, in the USA, were not to be underestimated.

When *Car & Driver* tested a 264 in April 1976 there was no doubt in the minds of its testers what the Volvo's strengths were and its review also brought home the massive difference in expectations between European and American buyers. Whereas the 240 and 260 series were seen as pretty large cars in Europe, by the time they had travelled to America they were perceived as compacts. A Cadillac may have cost the same, but it offered a huge amount of metal.

As *Car & Driver* put it: 'The 264 resembles every Volvo of the last 10 years, and the all-new front makes the car look like a razor with headlights'. As had become expected in any Volvo review, the verdict was that this was a car for those who put function above style and who weren't interested in impressing the neighbours.

There was a new 1,986cc version of the B21 engine for 1977, which was fitted to the 244L. Rated at 90bhp and known as the B19 unit, this was offered for drivers who needed to specify a car with an engine of less then two litres for tax purposes. This year also marked the company's 50th anniversary, and considering the popularity that the company had enjoyed in previous decades it is a shame that in 1977 it was having a hard time, to say the least. Global production had fallen from 296,800 to 225,700 and in an attempt to reduce the enormous number of cars which had been stockpiled as a result of the fall in sales, production was cut. Swedish sales alone were down from 76,600 in 1976 to just 55,700 in 1977 – a drop of over 27 per cent. As well as the increase in popularity of other car companies' products, and the increase in showroom prices of Volvo's cars, the company's reputation for durable products had taken a battering since the introduction of the 240 and 260.

It had not taken long for it to become evident that the

The PRV joint venture

One of the first big deals that new Volvo chairman Pehr Gyllenhammar would get involved in was the setting up of a new company with Renault and Peugeot. Despite the fact that Gyllenhammar assumed his post in May 1971, the deal was signed on 29 June 1971 – pretty fast moving by anybody's standards. The new company was called *Societe Franco-Suedoise des Motors* PRV and it was a venture aimed at developing a completely new engine and sharing the costs.

The initial plan was to build a 3.5-litre 90° V8 with alloy heads and an alloy block. The powerplant would be used for all three companies to install in their most expensive cars but having ordered all the costly machinery that would be installed at the new, purpose-built factory in Douvrin, the triumvirate realised they had made a mistake. Market projections suggested the demand would not be there for such a car, so the decision was made to chop a pair of cylinders off the end and turn it into a V6, the definitive size for which would be 2,664cc.

Despite pooling resources to develop the new engine, the three manufacturers would compete with each other in the marketplace. The factory was geared up to produce 350,000 engines annually and for Volvo the first of its cars to receive the new powerplant was the 1974 264, which used the 140bhp B27 engine. Meanwhile, Peugeot would first fit the engine to its 604 and Talbot Tagora while Renault would use the engine in its 30. The co-operative continued right up until 1990 when the 960 was launched with an all-new in-line six-cylinder engine.

rustproofing of these cars was not up to Volvo's usual high standards, and within months many cars were starting to corrode. Having spent several decades building an image of incredible durability, it was in danger of being thrown away in a matter of months. The independent Swedish Motor Vehicle Inspection Company had done an audit of different cars on the market in the mid-1970s and Volvo's vehicles had come out on top with an average life expectancy of 16 years – far in advance of most other cars. However, it did not take long to see that the new models wouldn't match this figure unless drastic action was taken to rectify the situation. Volvo offered resprays to owners whose cars were affected by premature rusting. It cost Volvo a huge amount of money, but it also restored faith in the company and its products, and that was more important than taking the short-term view that would have been adopted by most of Volvo's rivals.

Despite all this hard work that went into bolstering the company's reputation, its cars were still cursed with a negative image. Safety and durability were obviously still major selling points, but other cars were starting to come along which offered these benefits together with at least a modicum of style. Something more radical than a minor tweak here and there was needed, but such developments would take time so in the meantime the occasional nip-and-tuck would have to suffice until a substantially new car could be launched to replace the 240 and 260 series. For 1978, there was a new sporty derivative, the 242GT. Using the 123bhp B21E engine, this was a two-door saloon with a distinctly sporting flavour thanks to 20-spoke alloy wheels, front fog lamps and a black interior with red pinstriping. Silver paintwork was lifted with black and orange striping and stiffer dampers were fitted so that the car could be driven more enthusiastically. The tactic worked. 'This is a Volvo even a car lover could love' wrote *Car & Driver*. 'This one makes a

statement. It is a sporty car. Sporty to look at and sporty to drive'. At last, here was a Volvo that lasted forever, but was enjoyable enough to drive for a car enthusiast to want to buy.

The rear end styling was altered in 1978 to feature wraparound lamps and an enlarged bootlid. At the same time, the front-end styling was tidied up, with square headlamps in place of the previous circular units. It wasn't all cosmetic though as the suspension was also tuned to improve handling. Stiffer anti-roll bars and dampers were the extent of the changes, but that made quite a difference to the car's dynamics. These changes were perhaps most beneficial to the sporty 242GT and when that car received the B23 engine it was even better than the outgoing car thanks to having an extra 17bhp (there was now 140bhp on tap) courtesy of a 2,315cc powerplant.

The main development for the 1979 range was the introduction of Volvo's first production diesel car. Developed in conjunction with Volkswagen, the D24 engine was the world's first six-cylinder diesel powerplant for use in a passenger

The introduction of the 164 had allowed people to trade up from a 140 series but still keep a Volvo on their drive, so it made sense to offer a six-cylinder version of the 240 series.

car. Displacing 2,383cc, this overhead cam unit featured an aluminium cylinder head and developed 82bhp, but the figures weren't the important thing – what made the engine such a winner was its refinement. Volvo had paid for the exclusive use of this powerplant, which was basically a six-cylinder version of the VW/Audi five-cylinder unit, but when *Road & Track* compared the oil-burning Volvo with competition from Peugeot and Audi it was beaten by both overall – despite Audi's 5000 using the five-cylinder version of the same engine. Clearly, the engine alone was not enough to win the day – the rest of the driving experience was important and Volvo just hadn't paid enough attention to it.

Also introduced in 1979 was the luxury version of the 240 range – the GLT which had a choice of either the four-cylinder 140bhp B23E engine or a 141bhp PRV V6 engine, although

The four-door saloon derivatives of the 240 series were always overshadowed by their more practical estate car counterparts.

If it had not been for the estate version of the 240 series, there is a good chance that the range might have been killed off much earlier than it was. This is a 1984 model.

estate buyers could opt only for the latter. The premise of the GLT was that it offered both luxury and a sporting drive, thanks to higher equipment levels with such details as alloy wheels and lower-profile tyres. Initially, the V6 engine displaced 2,664cc but from 1981 it gained 14bhp because of an increase in capacity to 2,849cc, becoming the B28E in the process.

At the same time, Volvo went all-out to produce a truly sporting 240 with the introduction of the 244 Turbo. Using a fuel-injected B21E powerplant with a Garrett turbocharger, the 155bhp generated was enough to take the car to 119mph (191kph) – around 7mph (11kph) faster than the 2.3-litre GLT. Although it seemed a bit late in the day for much cosmetic development of the car, the bumpers were significantly reduced in size at the same time so it didn't look as ungainly.

In 1982, the 760 arrived: Volvo's attempt at taking its range further

upmarket. With a trio of six-cylinder engines or a turbocharged four, it was clear that there was too much overlap with the 260 range. Although the 264 was a little too close in concept to the 760, it was another three years before production ceased, with the last car being built in 1985. In that year, with an annual production of 414,700 cars, more than a quarter of Volvo's output was of the 240 range, with sales in 1985 totalling no fewer than 120,800.

From the introduction of the 760 through to the demise of the 240, there was relatively little development of the latter range, but from the end of 1982 the 242, 244 and 245 badges gave way to a straightforward 240 series tag, the range being offered with a choice of three engines and manual or automatic transmissions. At the same time, the range received a minor facelift with a restyled bonnet, different headlamps and an amended grille, from then, through to the car's demise it was a case of extra pieces of equipment being added to the specification list, and little more. Yet this lack of development meant little, as the 240 became a cult car, especially popular in estate form with antique dealers, thanks to its cavernous cargo bay. Car reviewers

may have avoided them (there was virtually no UK press coverage of the 240 range after 1981), but it made no difference – sales continued to boom which is why Volvo just couldn't pull the plug. Time had to be called on the car at some point, and on 5 May 1993, the last 240 was built. A green estate, this was the end of an era because the car had been produced for 19 years, nearly 2.7 million rolling off the production lines in that time.

Bertone was commissioned in 1976 to build a six-seater version of the 264. Based on the 264GL, the result was the 264TE, complete with telephone and a fridge.

Buying a 240 or 260

1. Although these cars have a reputation for lasting, the newest examples are now over a decade old, with the oldest three times that. The bodywork may take neglect more readily than other cars will, but on abused examples there's a good chance the wheel-arches, rear damper mountings, sills and wings will have started to rust. As long as you carry out the standard basic checks that you should for any car, you are unlikely to get caught out by a car harbouring serious rot.

2. Engines are long-lived which ever version you buy, whether it has four cylinders or six. As long as the oil and filter have been changed regularly they will all clock up 200,000 miles quite happily. Transmissions are just the same, with manual and automatic gearboxes able to take a quarter of a million miles without fuss. It's worth making sure the fluid in the automatic transmission is red – if it's black or brown the unit will need to be replaced soon.

The 262C

The demise of the 1800ES in the summer of 1973 meant that Volvo no longer had a stylish coupé in its line up. Although producing a distinctly separate model from the current range was not going to be possible, there was the option of building a two-door luxury saloon with a coupé roof-line. Jan Wilsgaard was tasked with producing designs for a coupé version of the 260 series and this was the car which became the ill-fated 262 coupé launched in 1976.

If Volvo wanted to offer a model which was perceived as exclusive, it would have to do better than merely producing a two-door version of its 264. Something more bespoke was needed and once Wilsgaard had come up with a new design, with a bit of help from design house Coggiola, Bertone built the car for Volvo which didn't have the facility to assemble it. The new car featured a roofline considerably altered from the standard model, trimmed with a vinyl roof and packed with luxury equipment inside. The prototype cars featured a three-crown logo behind the side windows – during

development the car had been codenamed Tre Kronor, or Three Crowns, but for the production model, which made its debut in Spring 1977, there was just a single crown and a Bertone badge at the rear of the front wings.

All 262Cs were fitted with the PRV engine, at first in 2664cc 140bhp form. This was enough to give the car a top speed of 106mph (170kph), which may not have been especially quick, but it was the comfort and refinement which went with it that made the 262C desirable.

Unfortunately, the lines haven't aged very well (even when current there were many who felt the proportions were a long way out), but when available new, it was seen as a stylish and desirable car by many. *Road & Track*'s verdict was that the 262C sounded similar to a Maserati Merak when given its head and although Volvo's prices had climbed steeply in recent years, the car still represented good value on account of its exclusivity and amazingly long list of standard equipment. With 1,000 of the first year's production of 1,200 going to the States it was important that the car received favourable US

press coverage. It was therefore unfortunate that *Car & Driver* was rather less than enthusiastic about Bertone's new baby. Their verdict was that the car was cramped and nothing like as enjoyable to drive as it should have been with a $15,995 price tag.

Because the 262C was based on the 264, its development mirrored that of the 264. This meant the rear end styling was changed in the autumn of 1978 to incorporate the new rear lights and in the summer of 1980 production was halted briefly while production was switched to incorporate a new front-end design. At first, all cars were painted silver and fitted with a black vinyl roof but from 1979 there was the option of gold paintwork and a painted steel roof. The original intention had been to produce just 800 cars annually over a period of four years, but as the car proved to be more popular than that, despite its very mixed reception, no fewer than 6,622 examples had rolled off the production lines by the time the last example was built. Of these, around three quarters were exported to the USA while just 200 found owners in Sweden.

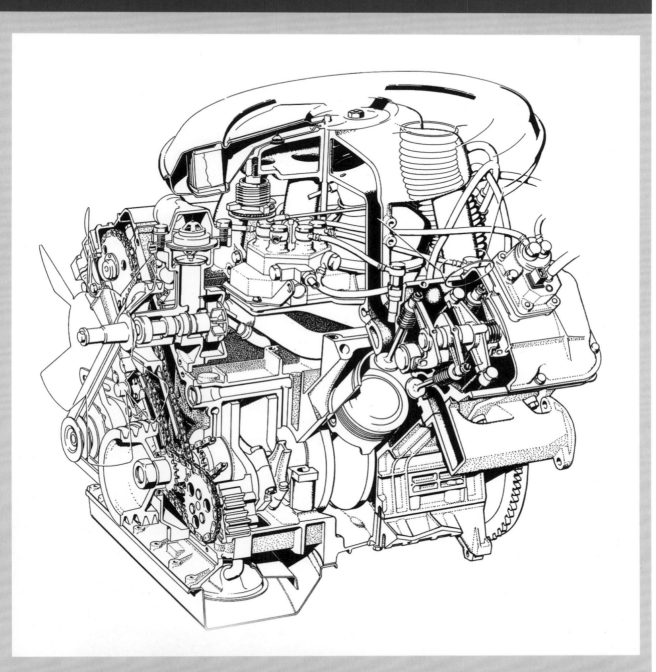

Left: Its proportions look ill-judged now, but when the 262C was launched it was a stylish flagship for Volvo – yet it still didn't sell in big numbers.

Above: Volvo B27 engine cutaway.

The Daf *acquisition* and the 300 series

As early as the late 1960s, Volvo had been eyeing up Daf in the Netherlands with a view to a merger. With both companies producing heavy commercial vehicles in the same sector, it made sense to share resources rather than compete with each other, but Daf had other ideas. It wasn't its truck division which it wanted to share with Volvo, but its car manufacturing facility. In 1969, the Van Doorne family which

headed Daf, approached Volvo with a view to taking over their car-building business. At that time, Hakan Frisinger was president of the Volvo Car Corporation and after a year of studying Daf's car-making business he concluded that Volvo was better off not getting involved.

Within a year however, everything had changed. Volvo had a new president in Pehr Gyllenhammar and Daf had made some changes to the

It took a lot of development by Volvo before the Daf 55 could be turned into the Volvo 66; it wasn't a case of just sticking on Volvo badges!

66

1975–1980

ENGINE:
Four cylinders in-line, iron block and alloy head

Bore x stroke	73mm x 77mm
Capacity	1,289cc
Valvegear	Overhead-valve
Compression ratio	8.5:1
Fuelling	Single Solex carburettor
Maximum power	57bhp (DIN) at 5,000rpm
Maximum torque	61lb ft at 2,800rpm

TRANSMISSION:
Rear-wheel-drive
Continuously variable transmission

SUSPENSION:
Front: Independent with longitudinal torsion bars, MacPherson struts, trailing links, anti-roll bar
Rear: De Dion rigid axle, semi-elliptic leaf-springs, upper torque arms, telescopic dampers

STEERING:

Type	Rack-and-pinion
Turns lock-to-lock	3.4

BRAKES:

Front:	Disc
Rear:	Drum

Servo assistance standard

WHEELS/TYRES:
4.0in pressed-steel wheels with 135 SR14 tyres

BODYWORK:
All-steel monocoque
Two-door saloon, three-door estate

DIMENSIONS:

Length	12ft 10in (3.90m)
Wheelbase	7ft 4in (2.25m)
Track – front	4ft 4in (1.31m)
Track – rear	4ft 1in (1.24m)
Width	5ft 0in (1.54m)
Height	4ft 6in (1.38m)

WEIGHT:
1,797lb (815kg)

PERFORMANCE: (Source: Volvo)

Max speed	85mph
0–50mph	12.9sec

UK PRICE WHEN NEW (February 1976):

Three-door hatchback	£1,945
Three-door estate	£2,095

NUMBER MADE:

Total	106,137 (plus 146,297 Daf 66s)
Saloons	77,637
Estates	28,500

NOTES:
There was also an 1,108cc version of the 66 which was not available in the UK and base models (the 66L) were fitted with drum brakes all round.

343

1976–1984

ENGINE:
Four cylinders in line, iron block and alloy head

Bore x stroke	76mm x 77mm
Capacity	1,397cc
Valvegear	Overhead-valve
Compression ratio	9.5:1
Fuelling	Single Weber carburettor
Maximum power	70bhp (DIN) at 5,500rpm
Maximum torque	80lb ft at 3,500rpm

TRANSMISSION:
Rear-wheel-drive
Variomatic continuously variable transmission

Final drive ratio:	3.91:1

SUSPENSION:
Front: Independent with coil springs, telescopic dampers, wishbones, anti-roll bar
Rear: Transaxle with De Dion rear axle, leaf springs and telescopic shock absorbers

STEERING:
Unassisted rack-and-pinion

Turns lock-to-lock	4.10

BRAKES:

Front:	Discs
Rear:	Drums

Standard servo assistance

WHEELS/TYRES:
4.5in wheels with 155 SR13 tyres

BODYWORK:
All-steel monocoque
Three-door hatchback, five-door hatchback from 1980

DIMENSIONS:

Length	13ft 8in (4.19m)
Wheelbase	7ft 10in (2.39m)
Track	4ft 5in (1.35m)
Width	5ft 5in (1.66m)
Height	4ft 6in (1.39m)
WEIGHT:	2,156lb (978kg)

PERFORMANCE: (Source: Motor)

Max speed	91mph
0–60mph	14.1sec
30–50mph in top	11.3sec
50–70mph in top	14.2sec

UK PRICE WHEN NEW (December 1978):

Three-door hatchback	£3,350

NUMBER MADE:

300 series three-door	505,969
300 series four-door	146,171
300 series five-door	434,266

360

1982–1989

As 343 except:
ENGINE:
Four cylinders in line, iron block and alloy head

Bore x stroke:	88.9mm x 88.0mm
Capacity	1,986cc
Valvegear	Overhead-cam
Compression ratio	10.0:1
Fuelling	Bosch fuel injection
Maximum power	115bhp (DIN) at 6,000rpm
Maximum torque	118lb ft at 3,600rpm

TRANSMISSION:
Five-speed manual

Final drive ratio	3.64:1

SUSPENSION:
Front: Independent with MacPherson struts, anti-roll bar
Rear: Transaxle with De Dion rear axle, leaf springs and telescopic shock absorbers

STEERING:
Unassisted rack-and-pinion

Turns lock-to-lock	4.25

WHEELS/TYRES:
5.5in wheels with 185/60 R14 tyres

BODYWORK:
Five-door hatchback; four-door from 1983

DIMENSIONS:

Length	14ft 1in (4.3m)
Wheelbase	7ft 10in (2.39m)
Track	4ft 5in (1.35m)
Width	5ft 5in (1.66m)
Height	4ft 6in (1.39m)

WEIGHT:
2,517lb (1,142kg)

PERFORMANCE: (Source: Autocar)

Max speed	112mph
0–60mph	11.1sec
30–50mph in top	14.8sec
50–70mph in top	14.9sec

UK PRICE WHEN NEW (December 1982):

Five-door hatchback	£6,548

55, with it becoming the 66. Sales had increased and the Daf operation was now profitable. Gyllenhammar was keen to expand Volvo and acquiring Daf was a quick way of achieving that, so on 1 January 1973 Volvo became the owner of one third of Daf. At first the cars retained Daf badging, while the build quality was improved to Volvo levels. The first Dafs built after the Volvo take over were still pretty shoddily made and damaging the reputation of the parent company would have been a real possibility if Volvo badges had been used instead. In 1971 and '72, the Swedish Motor Vehicle Inspection Company had reported that the Daf was among the lowest quality cars on sale in Sweden at that time, with bodyshell defects and very poorly constructed exhaust systems –

certainly not a car that was worthy of being associated closely with the Volvo name.

The result was some rapid re-engineering of the car with much better interior trim, a new dash, more thorough anti-rust measures and higher quality fixtures and fittings. By the summer of 1975 the Daf name gave way to Volvo's, with the 66 looking like a Swedish product rather than a Dutch one from then on. The name change coincided with the acquisition of a further 42 per cent of Daf by Volvo, along with the car production facility at Born in the Netherlands. To mark the change of ownership the grille fitted to the cars featured the Volvo stripe while the bumpers became 'safety' items, but the very strange suspension remained, with a somewhat odd

The Daf 55 Marathon coupé.

DAF background

Although Daf had been making commercial trailers since 1928, the Dutch company did not start producing cars until 1959, having shown its first car, the 22bhp 590cc Daf 600, at the Amsterdam Exhibition of 1958. By the end of the 1960s around 65,000 examples were rolling off the production lines each year, which was about a third of the number of cars Volvo was producing. From the outset, the 600 had Daf's novel belt-driven transmission – the Variomatic. In recent years this has become known as the CVT (continuously variable transmission) and it allows an engine to run at more or less peak torque for the conditions for much of the time. Because the transmission was so simple and reliable it had been used to great effect in a light military truck and even a Formula 3 car, as well as numerous rally cars which Daf campaigned successfully.

Although the new transmission was greeted with much scepticism, the car proved reasonably successful for Daf and in 1962 the more powerful (30bhp) 750 – and a deluxe version called the Daffodil – were launched, still using the Variomatic transmission. In 1967, the 750 was renamed the 33 and it was joined by the Michelotti-styled 44, powered by a 40bhp 844cc version of Daf's own air-cooled flat-twin engine. Within a year, the 55 was on sale, using the same bodyshell as the 44 but with an even bigger engine, in this case a 50bhp 1,108cc Renault four-cylinder unit. To supplement the saloon bodystyle, an estate and a charming coupé were also available. Building on its motorsport successes there was even a sport version of this, called the Marathon. With 55bhp available from the 1,108cc four-cylinder engine, the Marathon could crack 85mph (137kph).

For 1972, there was a new centrifugal clutch and a De Dion back axle to replace the swing axle suspension previously fitted, while at the same time the designation 66 was adopted in place of the 55 tag. Saloons and estates continued to be offered alongside each other and for the Dutch armed forces there was a cabriolet version. A major development for the company was that in 1972 Volvo acquired 33.3 per cent of Daf's shares, which was increased to 75 per cent in 1974. As a result, Daf dealers were able to sell Volvo cars from that year, but by the following year the Daf name had disappeared altogether from cars, the 66 by now appearing with a Volvo badge.

The mergers that didn't happen

The 1970s was a very unstable decade for Volvo, just as it was for most other car manufacturers. As a result, the company was always looking at opportunities to share resources and expand its operations.

In May 1977, the boards of Volvo and Saab announced that they were to merge, to form a new company called Volvo-Saab Scania AB which would be headed by Pehr Gyllenhammar, CEO of Volvo. The overcapacity that ran throughout the car manufacturing industry during the 1970s, along with the erratic economic fortunes of the developed world, made such a proposition attractive.

By pooling resources it was estimated that billions of kronor could be saved – platforms could be shared, parts could be bought in or manufactured in greater quantities and instead of investing in two models for the same sector it would be possible to develop just one.

It soon became clear to the directors of Saab that Volvo would be the dominant partner (despite the agreement being that it would be a merger rather than a takeover) and less than three months later it was announced that the deal was off, the management of Volvo having decided that they could wait no longer for the members of the executive board of Saab-Scania to make up their minds.

Pehr Gyllenhammar was still keen to expand however, and he set up talks with the Norwegian government to see if they would be keen on financing the company. The talks were made public in May 1978 when it was announced that in return for SKr750m, Norway would get a 40 per cent share of Volvo. The deal was signed in December 1978, but within weeks the company's shareholders were furious about the proposals and were insistent that such a deal should never happen. They got their way, and the whole deal was called off.

system at the front. Daf described it as using longitudinal torsion bars with an anti-roll bar and telescopic double-acting hydraulic shock absorbers, also acting as kingpins. At the rear, there was De Dion rear suspension in which half-elliptic rear springs supported the car, and where the De Dion tube linking the rear wheels ran behind the Variomatic final drive. This was a major advance over the suspension used in the 55, as on that car the independent rear suspension was by swing axles and coil springs, which meant that the rear-mounted belt-drive pulleys had to articulate with the swinging half axles. Not only did that cause problems with the alignment of the belts, which led to premature wear, but it was also the reason for sometimes vicious oversteer which could make the car's handling unpredictable.

By the end of 1975, Daf Cars was just a memory with the 66 doing reasonably well for Volvo despite reviews of the car pointing out that it was not as refined as it should be considering it cost around £2,000. Not only that, but the 66 was underpowered although the most pressing problem for Volvo at that time wasn't the ironing out of the 66's faults, it was addressing the issue of having a 1.3-litre entry-level car with nothing between that and a 2.1-litre luxury vehicle – a big step up from its sibling. What was needed was something to fill the gap, and it just so happened that Daf had been working on such a car.

This new model was a development of the existing 66 and initially it was proposed that it would be badged the 77. Using a Renault 1,397cc engine, it was ideal for Volvo as it slotted into the bottom of its range. Jan Wilsgaard was asked to choose between a proposal put forward by Trevor Fiore and the project on which Daf had been working. Although Wilsgaard wasn't desperately keen on either of the proposals, he felt there was more mileage in opting for the Daf one, but modifying it as much as possible. However, as the project was already quite far advanced there wasn't as much room for manoeuvre as he would have liked. So, although Trevor Fiore has been credited with designing the 340

series, it was actually a much-modified Daf design.

The result was the 343, so named because it was the third car developed since the 121 in the mid-1950s, it had a four-cylinder engine and three doors. It has been the butt of jokes ever since it was launched at the 1976 Geneva Motor Show as the specification of the car was something that many people simply did not understand. Here was a mid-size car with a belt-driven transmission (the CVT system) while under the bonnet there was an engine displacing a mere 1,397cc. Not only was the Renault engine getting long in the tooth by that stage, but there was no room for increasing the engine's capacity, so when it became apparent that the performance was on the lukewarm side of dull, there would be no

The introduction of a five-door 340 was crucial in ensuring a growth in sales for Volvo's small car. The plan worked.

Early examples of the 343 were problematic, with all sorts of complaints from buyers. Volvo resolved those it could however, to turn the car's fortunes around.

option but to re-engineer the car to take a completely different powerplant.

As if that weren't enough, the economy wasn't too great either. Add a high price into the mix – partly because of the exchange rate – and Volvo seemed to be on a hiding to nothing.

The front end, with MacPherson struts and the De Dion rear end with single-element leaf springs was an evolution of the 66 set-up, as was the rack-and-pinion steering; the brakes were discs at the front and drums at the rear. But it wasn't only the technical specification and the styling which were conservative; so were the colour choices. It did not matter which of the five exterior colours was chosen (green, brown, beige, red or yellow) you would have to have a brown interior whether you liked it or not. Over the next two years it was clear that Volvo's new baby was not proving popular, a situation not helped by several recalls in the early stages of the car's life. Dutch car production went down sharply, reflecting the lack of sales – despite the saloon version of the 66 being in production up until 1980, and still averaging 14,000

sales a year. Buyers and the press found fault with just about every aspect of the car it seemed, criticising its engine, transmission, poor heating, cramped interior, and poor build quality. The answer was to embark on a wide-ranging quality-improvement programme as well as to offer a conventional manual transmission, this arriving in the autumn of 1978. Reviews of the 343 were still somewhat mixed, but when *Autocar* compared a Variomatic-equipped 343 with its manual gearbox counterpart, the improvement was clear – acceleration and economy were way ahead even though the manual gearbox wasn't that pleasant to use.

To free up some capital so that the car could be developed, Volvo had reduced its stake in Daf from 75 per cent to 55 per cent. Initially, the Van Doorne family retained an interest in the company but when Volvo reduced its interest it was the Dutch government which bought all the available shares. Volvo retained a controlling stake in Daf, but the Dutch government, which now held the other 45 per cent of the shares, was able to inject some much-needed cash into the company so that the 300 series could be developed properly.

In 1976, the motorsport craze was rallycross, and although Volvo wasn't focusing especially heavily on motorsport at that time, the

decision was made to begin a series called the Volvo Rallycross Cup. Almost immediately the series proved incredibly popular with drivers and spectators and for the next five years the series was to prove one of the most popular forms of motorsport. Because the 343 hadn't got off to a great start in terms of the image it portrayed – potential buyers were still being put off by early recalls – it was decided to enter a team of 343s in the rallycross series.

At that stage there were no obvious drivers to choose for the 343 team, with the exception of one man. This was Per-Inge 'PI' Walfridson, who was the son of a Volvo dealer and already one of Sweden's leading rally drivers. Keen to try his hand at rallycross, Walfridson signed up for the job and got off to an excellent start by winning the most important races in the series. In fact, he did so well that, in 1978, Volvo decided to expand its rallycross division and go out into Europe, renaming Volvo Competition Service as Volvo R-Sport, with the drivers known as the R-team. By 1980, there were four drivers in the team, Walfridson was European champion and the other drivers had taken third, fourth and fifth places. Having enjoyed great success, but with the popularity of rallycross starting to wane, there was little point in continuing to fund the team and Volvo decided to

XD-1 – the diesel 343

Veteran Volvo rally driver, Carl-Magnus Skogh, had the novel idea of attempting the world diesel land speed record using a 343. In Finland the company marketed a five-cylinder diesel unit which displaced just under two litres, and it was this engine that was used for the record attempt. A plastic body was

constructed and ditching anything that wasn't necessary, led to a 440lb (200kg) reduction in kerb weight. By the time a turbocharger had been fitted (to give a 140bhp power output) to the 343, the 1,980lb (900kg) car, badged XD-1, was ready.

So one morning in 1978, Skogh attempted the record at Landvetter

airport, between planes taking off and landing. He had already cracked 144mph (232kph) during testing and the record was just 128mph (206kph), but conditions were poor and the best he could achieve on the official runs was 131mph (211kph) – still enough to clinch the record.

The Variomatic transmission

While there are those who must have the latest innovation, it is more usual for emerging technologies to receive short shrift until they have proved that they really are an advance on prevailing systems. And so it was for the Variomatic transmission, which many saw as unnecessarily complicated while delivering an end result that wasn't much of an advance over a conventional automatic gearbox.

When it was announced, there were few small cars with automatic transmissions, and for those who preferred the gears to shift themselves, it was just the thing – simple to use and of straightforward design, the Variomatic had two fundamental points in its favour. With further development, the technology has proved to be worthwhile, with continuously variable transmissions now used by many manufacturers such as Nissan, MG-Rover and Ford.

The principle behind the Variomatic transmission is that of maximising the engine's efficiency by allowing it to always be turning at optimum revs, pretty much regardless of the car's road speed. By altering the gearing seamlessly rather than in steps, it is then possible always to have exactly the right gear rather than one which might be just too high or fractionally too low.

To help market the transmission, Daf compared Variomatic with conventional automatic gearboxes and claimed that its new system solved all the problems of normal self-shifting transmissions at a stroke. Problems such as poor fuel consumption, high maintenance costs and a lack of driver control were all inherent in the usual automatic gearbox, but according to Daf the Variomatic did not suffer from these problems. Of course, the reality was that most of these traits remained, but the advantage of ease of use also remained and for some drivers that was enough to give the Variomatic-equipped Daf a try.

There were some aspects of the Variomatic which were a genuine advance, such as the ability for the

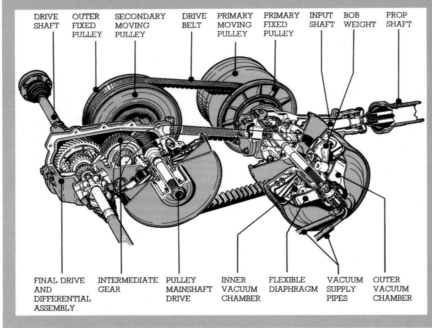

DRIVE SHAFT • OUTER FIXED PULLEY • SECONDARY MOVING PULLEY • DRIVE BELT • PRIMARY MOVING PULLEY • PRIMARY FIXED PULLEY • INPUT SHAFT • BOB WEIGHT • PROP SHAFT

FINAL DRIVE AND DIFFERENTIAL ASSEMBLY • INTERMEDIATE GEAR • PULLEY MAINSHAFT DRIVE • INNER VACUUM CHAMBER • FLEXIBLE DIAPHRAGM • VACUUM SUPPLY PIPES • OUTER VACUUM CHAMBER

withdraw from European racing for a while, but the series had done its job, with things having picked up almost immediately for the 343. The press had started writing far more positive things about the car – What Car? claimed in 1978 that the 343 was the 'most improved car of the year'. Greater economy, better acceleration and a higher top speed were all provided by the swap to a manual gearbox and Volvo could also sell the car for £200 less than the CVT version. At last it was on to a winner.

With quality now under control it was time to expand the range, to hook more buyers. The 240-sourced manual gearbox was proving very popular (by 1982 just 15 per cent of 340s were sold with the CVT system) and a choice of trim levels led to increased sales. There was even a special edition in 1978 called the Black Beauty on account of it being available only in black with a red stripe, alloy wheels and tinted glass. Soon after, the 343L and the 343GL joined the 343DL, which until then, had been the sole model on

offer. The new arrivals offered lower and higher equipment levels respectively. In 1979, an extra pair of doors joined the options list – a car of this size always needed a five-door option, and being able to offer one meant many buyers found the car more appealing.

There were still flies in the ointment though because two of the biggest original bugbears that the press and the public had with the first 343s were the underpowered engine and the appallingly cramped rear seat. The latter problem was gear lever to stay in drive all the time, without the car creeping forward when traffic ground to a halt. This was thanks to a centrifugal clutch, and this arrangement also meant that the Daf could be towed if necessary – which is not the case with a normal automatic. However perhaps the main advantage of the transmission is its ability to ensure that the engine is running either at or near peak torque levels virtually all the time, allowing it to run as efficiently as possible while also maintaining optimum performance.

The key to the Variomatic transmission is a pair of belts which transmit drive from one a pair of driving pulleys to a pair of driven pulleys. By varying the operating diameter of the pulleys the gear ratio can be adjusted so that the engine can be kept at optimum revs. The driving pulleys are turned by the engine while the driven ones are mounted on a cross shaft so that they can turn the final drive.

Each of the pulleys is made in two halves, with one half fixed to its shaft and the other free to slide along it. The face of each half is conical, so that the space between the two halves forms a deep V-section. The belts themselves have a slight wedge-shaped section

and they therefore fit into the space between the pulley halves. When the two halves are close together the belt seats itself near the pulley's outer edge, but as the sliding half moves away, the V of the pulley will slide deeper into it, thus reducing the effective diameter of the pulley.

Hence, when a high level of torque is required, the two halves of the driving pulleys are far apart so that the gearing is low, but as the car speeds up and the amount of torque needed is reduced, they move closer

There's no transmission quite like a Variomatic, although the principles of van Doorne's transmission survive in the modern CVT system.

together and the gearing is raised. At the same time the two halves of each of the driven pulleys will be doing the opposite, so that the ratio can be adjusted more quickly.

caused by the rear-mounted Variomatic transmission, which robbed the rear seat of valuable space. Fixing the problem meant a new floorpan and such changes were not something that could be put right quickly. At least the weedy engine could be easily remedied as it was simply a case of fitting a larger unit, but fixing the floorpan needed a major injection of cash. Luckily for Volvo, the Dutch government was keen to increase its stake in the Dutch arm of the company and it made money available for product

development from 1979 right through to 1986.

The solution to the underpowered engine was the fitment of the B19A 1,986cc powerplant from the 240 series, with the car becoming known as the 360 in the process. This happened in the summer of 1980 but it was reserved for certain markets only – the UK not being one of them. That market had to wait until late 1982, which was also when the 343 and 345 tags were dropped, the car becoming known simply as the 340. A year previously, the car received its

first significant facelift which consisted of new front-end styling with modified panelwork and lights. The next big improvement was the availability of a 1,720cc overhead-cam Renault engine, to sell alongside the 1,397cc model. The 2-litre engine in particular was a welcome addition to the range, and with high equipment levels as well (including a five-speed manual gearbox as standard), the 360 was worthy of the Volvo name insofar as it was the luxury option for those who wanted a small car, but without a small car feel.

The Bertone Tundra

By the time the Bertone Tundra made its debut at the 1979 Geneva Motor Show, the Italian coachbuilder had already been enjoying a fruitful relationship with Volvo for several years with production of the 262C, manufacture of which had started in 1977. By basing the Tundra on a manual-transmission 343, Volvo's entry-level model was cast back into the public eye and it also allowed Bertone to strengthen its link with the Swedish maker.

The boxy, angular lines of the Tundra didn't really appeal to many, the roofline, which extended down behind the doors, drawing much of the criticism. In hindsight, the Tundra looked much like a three-door version of the Citroën BX. The offset grille made the car look unbalanced – the aim had been to make housing the numberplate easier, but the design backfired.

With very slim pillars all round and flush-fitting glazing the car appeared to have an awful lot of glass and this also drew criticism, as in 1979, there were few who thought flush glazing would be commercially viable for perhaps decades to come. Of course, the reality was that within a decade many mass-market cars would have this feature.

Under the skin the car was more or less unchanged mechanically, the only difference being the adoption of shorter leaf springs for the De Dion rear suspension so that the car could be shortened by 7in (178mm) seven inches. The interior embraced the digital age which was just dawning at the end of the 1970s – an electronic dashboard featured a display which changed colour depending on whether or not everything was functioning correctly.

If everything was illuminated in green all was well – but a change to white meant there were problems somewhere.

When *Autocar* looked at the Tundra the feeling was that something very much like it would be seen pretty soon after in the Volvo range. After all, Bertone had built a concept which was nearly production ready and would need very few changes to make it to the showrooms, but by the start of the 1980s the Tundra was all but forgotten.

Based on the 300 series, the Bertone Tundra didn't progress beyond the concept stage which is a shame as it would have given Volvo's range a bit of much-needed glamour.

UK sales of the 340 and 360 series boomed, whereas customers in most other countries had grown tired of the model by the mid-1980s.

Another addition to the 300 series range was a four-door saloon which joined the line-up in Autumn 1983. The replacement for the 300 series came at the end of 1988 in the form of the 440, although the 340 and 360 continued to be sold until the summer of 1989. These cars may have been joked about throughout their existence, but they were a major money earner for Volvo, especially in the UK. The 300 series often appeared in the Top Ten thanks to a loyal band of buyers who did not want to buy poorly built British cars and who were keen to avoid buying Japanese. While the motoring press might have cheered at its demise, Volvo's British dealers most certainly didn't.

Concept cars
and design studies

The origins of the VESC were all too apparent, but at a time when most car makers were churning out safety cars, at least Volvo's example looked much like the production car – the 240 series.

The first of Volvo's in-house concept projects was started in the late 1960s and reached fruition in the early 1970s. At that time, safety cars were all the rage, and Volvo focused on building ideas cars which were practical and functional, but in most cases downright ugly. The VESC, which stood simply for Volvo Experimental Safety Car, was first displayed in

1972. By then, American legislation had led most domestic manufacturers to produce vehicles which tested safety ideas, but they were only a reaction to safety laws which were passed in 1970. Volvo's was a much more considered approach, building on the work the company had been doing for over two decades.

Included in the car's design were airbags for front and rear passengers,

anti-lock brakes, pop-up head restraints, energy-absorbing bumpers front and rear, and an automatic fuel supply cut-off in the event of an impact. The car was also engineered to withstand a 50mph (80kph) rear-end impact while also surviving a serious head-on impact as well as a major roll. Styling may not have been the car's strong point, but if you were going to have an accident you couldn't have chosen anything much better than one of these cars in which to have it.

As the 1970s progressed the focus moved towards fuel efficiency and alternatives to the internal-combustion engine. Volvo was not going to be left behind and in the autumn of 1976 the company unveiled a pair of un-named prototype electric cars. Smaller than anything the company had ever produced before, the vehicles had four doors and four seats. Yet despite their diminutive proportions they weighed in at 2,205lb, or exactly a tonne (1,000kg). Even a 343 was fractionally lighter! Push-button gearchanges and a degree of comfort were not enough and predictably (like all electrically propelled cars) there was never any prospect of Volvo's prototype going into series production. In fact, Volvo was really just toying with interior and exterior designs in the hope that at some point a decent alternative to the battery would be discovered. Of course we're still waiting for that day . . .

Just before these electric prototypes were first seen, Volvo took part in a competition staged by the Museum of Modern Art in New York to come up with a modern interpretation of the taxi. Volvo chose to construct a prototype taxi that combined accessibility, safety and kindness to the environment in one package, and the imaginatively named Experimental Taxi was the result. The exterior design was hardly the car's strongest point, but the vehicle was more significant than it seemed because it was actually Volvo's first front-wheel-drive car. It

was also its last, until the 480 appeared in 1985.

Under the bonnet of the Taxi was a six-cylinder diesel engine, designed especially for Volvo by Ricardo. The oil-burning design was chosen because of the then-current fuel crisis, and fuel economy was the number one priority for just about anybody buying a car at that time – and particularly taxi drivers. To ensure the car was as accessible as

Top: Retrospectively and unofficially badged the Elcar, this commuter vehicle was built to explore the potential of electric power for the car. Unfortunately, it proved rather limited.

Bottom: Intended as a Volvo taxi cab, the Taxi (Volvo liked straightforward names for its concepts!) was typically boxy, but infinitely practical.

The Venus Bilo

It is interesting to note that the first concept car ever is generally regarded as Buick's 1938 Y-Job. Futuristic in both design and engineering, the Y-Job survives and even now is seen at events around the world. However, half a decade before Buick's concept was first seen, a test bed from Volvo was shown, and although the company did not officially appear as the creator, Volvo was instrumental in its creation.

The first Volvo concept was not built by the company itself, but by an independent coachbuilder using a PV653 chassis. It was known as the Venus Bilo, although this tag seems to have been pinned on the car later. Unveiled during November 1933, its designer was Gustaf Ericsson and the car was built by Stockholm-based Nordbergs Vagnafabrik.

Although at the time Volvo claimed to have no involvement in the project, it was later disclosed that the car had been built to test reactions to its advanced styling. As well as showing inspiration from contemporary aircraft design, interior space utilisation was also experimented with. Finished in

bright blue with beige stripes, the Venus Bilo also examined the idea of removable panels which could be replaced easily in the event of an accident.

Once on display the Venus Bilo drew a very mixed reaction. Most saw it as ugly and not conservative enough, although many agreed that the aerodynamic styling would become commonplace on cars of the future. In fact, one of Volvo's own cars benefited from the Venus Bilo's design, as the PV36 'Carioca' used

similar themes when it went into production in 1935. Although the car was never officially scrapped, nobody knows what has become of it since it was sold off in the late 1930s.

The Venus Bilo was so revolutionary when it was first seen in 1933 that Volvo didn't admit to being involved in the project! Despite its lack of popularity, Volvo put the Carioca into production just three years later.

possible for anybody who might need to travel in it, there was wheelchair access – made easier by the low floor. The wide, sliding door also made entry and exit easier while comfort once travelling was assured with air-conditioning as standard. The driver wasn't forgotten, with an automatic transmission to make life easier and in case a fare was picked up who decided to turn nasty, there was even bulletproof glass and a special payment hatch.

The next concept from Volvo was the VSCC, which was shown at the New York Motor Show in Spring 1978 and was developed by the US arm of Volvo. Otherwise known as the Volvo

Safety Concept Car, this was another test bed to gauge public reaction to such ideas as pulsating brake lights which flashed more quickly as the brakes were applied harder. Tyre pressure sensors were also incorporated as was a horn which became louder as the car travelled more quickly.

In Spring 1980, the public had its first taster of the car that would take Volvo through the 1980s and into the 1990s – the 700 series. Although there were differences, the VCC – for Volvo Concept Car – which was first seen at the 1980 Geneva Motor Show effectively provided a sneak preview. The company wanted to ensure that reaction to the car's styling wouldn't

be adverse, although if it had been, there was not that much that could be done about it as the production car had already been signed off. In the event, everybody who commented on the car seemed to just accept that Volvo would never worry about convention, and it would be something of a disappointment if the company had abandoned its angular lines just to fit in with everyone else.

Intended as a follow up to the 1976 electric prototypes, Volvo's eco-conscious concept of the 1980s was the LCP, or Light Component Project. Introduced in June 1983, a pair of cars were built, the first of which used a 1.3-litre three-cylinder

Within a couple of years the VCC would appear as a production car, although its proportions had been altered a fair bit in the transition to 700 series.

As the name suggests, the Lightweight Component Project (LCP) tested the viability of materials such as magnesium and aluminium in car manufacture.

Although the ECC was first shown in 1992, it did not reach the showroom until 1998, by which time it had become the S80. A dual-fuel version of the S80 is now available but the radical means of propulsion seen in the ECC did not make it into production.

direct-injection turbodiesel engine while the other car used a 1.4-litre turbodiesel. Although the motive power was clearly an important part of the project, the main rationale behind the car was to test lightweight materials such as magnesium, aluminium and various plastics which would not compromise safety, reliability or recyclability. The final weight of each car was just 700kg (1,543lb) and this, combined with careful attention to detail with the aerodynamics ensured the top speed was well over 100mph (160kph) while fuel consumption was miserly.

Although when it was launched, the design was radical, in the 21st century it is a car that wouldn't look too out of place, but whether or not buyers would be happy opting for a four-seater in which the rear-seat passengers face backwards is doubtful.

The Environmental Concept Car (ECC) was seen as far back as September 1992 and the S80 launched in 1998, looked suspiciously like it. The brief for this concept was

to design a car which offered quality, safety, comfort and performance, but which would also be environmentally friendly. The car's design would allow a drag coefficient of just 0.25, although in the event, the final result was a Cd of 0.23 – quite remarkable for a four-door saloon. The car also needed to be identifiably a Volvo, so it had to draw on styling themes from previous cars from the company. The Amazon's sides, the broad shoulders of the 144 and V-shape of the bonnet which had been a Volvo characteristic since the PV444 were all incorporated into the design.

With a bodyshell made of aluminium, intended to be fully recyclable, the ECC's light weight also aided fuel economy and performance. Within two years the Audi A8 was launched, complete with aluminium space frame, but there is still no sign of a Volvo being built which uses the same process although there's a good chance it could happen yet. Something else which proved to be something of a blind alley was the choice of a hybrid

Volvo has always placed safety and practicality before looks, but the 2000 Eyecar took this to extremes with a design that seems to be wilfully ugly.

powertrain. An electric/gas turbine system was chosen along with a two-speed automatic transmission, the 76bhp electric motor being used in urban driving and the 56bhp turbine saved for higher-speed driving. This allowed the ECC to reach 62mph (100kph) in 13 seconds and to achieve a top speed of 109mph (175kph), while burning up less fuel in gas turbine mode than a conventionally powered car. Carrying the HSG (high speed generator) tag, this means of propulsion allowed the car to drive as similarly as possible to a conventional car, but to have far less of an impact on the environment.

At the end of 2000, the Eyecar was unveiled, looking like a disfigured coupé version of the S80. It was called the Eyecar because the car's ergonomics were all very cleverly arranged around the eyes of the driver. This meant that seats, steering wheel, centre console and pedals all moved to suit the driver, but to make it even more impressive, the driver didn't even have to intervene as the car featured built-in sensors which detected where the driver's eyes were positioned and then moved everything to suit. The theory behind this was that optimum visibility was the key to making the roads safer, so by first positioning the eyes then adjusting everything else for the maximum comfort possible, accidents could be reduced. Perhaps in the car of the future that may become a production reality, but the B-pillars which arched inwards to increase visibility by reducing blindspots probably won't – they are

one of the reasons why the car looks so ungainly!

By the time the Safety Concept Car (SCC) was unveiled at the 2001 Detroit Auto Show, straight lines were banished, to be replaced by curves in every plane. The SCC looked essentially like an updated version of the 480ES while being rather more adventurous in its design – and packed the sort of technology and materials that were essential in any respectable concept of the new millennium. One of the unusual things about the car was that it looked like a three-door sports estate/coupé, but was actually a five-door car. The rear doors featured handles which looked as if they were a continuation of those fitted to the front doors and because the rear doors also slid backwards they were flush-fitting when closed. Also incorporated in

the SCC was the eye-controlled seating and pedal layout that had first been seen in the Eyecar. The vehicle itself was built by Italdesign, complete with semi-transparent A-pillars and very thin pillars elsewhere – again, to maximise all-round visibility.

Despite such excellent visibility being guaranteed, sensors were positioned within the door mirrors and rear bumper which would alert the driver to any hazards which appeared in the car's blind spots – or at least the areas which would be blind in a normal car. As if all this weren't enough, cameras supplemented the rear-view mirrors. Driving at night was also taken into account by incorporating a fibre optic headlamp design which allowed the light beam to be lengthened during high-speed driving or widened in urban areas.

Looking like a three-door sportshatch in the mould of the 1800ES, the SCC is actually a five-door hatch, and much better looking than most Volvo concepts.

The concept that became the XC90 SUV was originally shown as the Adventure Concept Car at the 2001 Detroit Auto Show.

The whole point of a concept car is to allow a manufacturer to test designs and technologies to see how acceptable they are to consumers – as well as to see if they actually work. On that basis, the Adventure Concept Car (ACC), which made its debut alongside the SCC at the 2001 Detroit Auto Show, was a resounding success. This was a taster of what Volvo's first foray into the sport utility vehicle (SUV) market would be like, and with the car now in production as the XC90, it is clear that the ACC was well received when first shown. When the concept first appeared, Volvo disclosed that it would be producing an SUV within two years, and the company was emphatic that it would not merely be a production version of the ACC. With the car now on sale it is clear that in reality, the showroom car shares much with the concept that spawned it – at least in terms of the basic design. To make sure that as much feedback as possible could be gathered by the product developers, a new website was set up (www.conceptlabvolvo.com) that enabled anybody to give their views on the ideas cars which were being unveiled by Volvo.

The 700 and 900 *series*

When the 700 series was launched, nobody sat on the fence about the new arrival. Most people hated the car's styling, but it still did extremely well for Volvo.

As far back as the mid-1970s, the management of Volvo had realised that if they did not start some major product development soon, the company would be in trouble. Even if they had begun developing a new car there and then it would be well into the 1980s before the fruits of their labours would be seen, so something had to be done, and fast. As a result, Jan Wilsgaard started to put some proposals together and before long he had around 50 sketches of cars which could conceivably become Volvo's all-new car to be launched in the early 1980s. Although the car was to have dimensions very similar to those of the 240, there would be much more interior space.

740

1984–1992

ENGINE:
Four cylinders in line, iron block and alloy head
Bore x stroke   96mm x 80mm
Capacity   2,316cc
Valvegear   Overhead camshaft
Compression ratio   10.3:1
Fuelling   Fuel injection
Maximum power   131bhp (DIN) at
                       5,400rpm
Maximum torque   140lb ft at 3,600rpm

TRANSMISSION:
Rear-wheel-drive
Four-speed manual with overdrive
Final drive ratio: 3.54:1

SUSPENSION:
Front: Independent with MacPherson struts,
coil springs, telescopic dampers, anti-roll bar
Rear: Live axle with trailing arms, coil springs,
telescopic dampers, Panhard rod

STEERING:
Assisted rack and pinion
Turns lock-to-lock   3.6

BRAKES:
Front & Rear: Discs
Standard servo assistance

WHEELS/TYRES:
5.5 x 14in pressed-steel wheels with 185/70
R14 tyres

BODYWORK:
All-steel monocoque
Four-door saloon (estate available from 1985)

DIMENSIONS:
Length   15ft 8½in (4.79m)
Wheelbase   9ft 1in (2.77m)
Track   4ft 9in (1.46m)
Width   5ft 9in (1.76m)
Height   4ft 8½in (1.41m)

WEIGHT: 2,812lb (1,272kg)

PERFORMANCE: (Source: *Autocar*)
Max speed   105mph
0–60mph   9.4sec
30–50mph in top   13.6sec
50–70mph in top   15.8sec

UK PRICE WHEN NEW (December 1984):
Four-door saloon   £12,796

NUMBER MADE:
740 saloon   650,443
740 estate   358,952
760 saloon   183,864
760 estate   37,445

NOTES:
The 760 saloon arrived first, in 1982. In 1984
the 740 saloon followed with estate versions
of both the 740 and 760 appearing in 1985.

760

1982–1990

As 740 except:
ENGINE:
Four cylinders in line, alloy block and head
Bore x stroke   91mm x 73mm
Capacity   2,849cc
Valvegear   Overhead cam
Compression ratio   9.5:1
Fuelling   Bosch K-Jetronic
                       fuel injection
Maximum power   156bhp (DIN) at
                       5,700rpm
Maximum torque   173lb ft at 3,000rpm

TRANSMISSION:
Three-speed automatic with overdrive

WHEELS/TYRES:
6 x 15in wheels with 195/60 HR15 tyres

WEIGHT: 3,024lb (1,373kg)

PERFORMANCE: (Source: *Autocar*)
Max speed   114mph
0–60mph   10.1sec
30–50mph in 1st   3.8sec
50–70mph in 2nd   6.1sec

UK PRICE INCLUDING TAX WHEN NEW
(October 1982):
Four-door saloon   £12,793

960

1990–1996

ENGINE:
Four cylinders in line, alloy block and head
Bore x stroke   83mm x 90mm

Capacity   2,922cc
Valvegear   Double overhead
                       camshaft
Compression ratio   10.7:1
Fuelling   Bosch Motronic
                       fuel injection
Maximum power   204bhp (DIN) at
                       6,000rpm
Maximum torque   197lb ft at 4,300rpm

TRANSMISSION:
Rear-wheel-drive
Four-speed automatic
Final drive ratio: 3.731 (without
                       overdrive)

SUSPENSION:
Front: Independent with MacPherson struts,
lower wishbones, coil springs, telescopic
dampers, anti-roll bar
Rear: Self-levelling telescopic dampers, anti-
roll bar

STEERING:
Assisted rack-and-pinion
Turns lock-to-lock   3.5

BRAKES:
Front: Ventilated disc
Rear: Disc
Standard servo assistance

WHEELS/TYRES:
6 x 15in alloy wheels with 195/65 R15 tyres

WEIGHT: 3,436lb (1,560kg)

PERFORMANCE: (Source: *Autocar*)
Max speed   128mph
0–60mph   9.3sec
30–50mph in top   3.4sec
50–70mph in top   4.8sec

UK PRICE WHEN NEW (November 1990):
Four-door saloon   £27,240

NUMBER MADE:
940 saloon   246,704
940 estate   231,677
960 saloon   112,710
960 estate   41,619

The 760's interior styling was much like the exterior – boxy and bland but it all worked well.

Twenty designs progressed to full-size drawings which were then reduced to eight full-scale clay models. Of these, a pair of designs were chosen for further development with mock-up interiors being created, and there was a major input from technical and marketing staff. The car was so important to Volvo that it did a huge amount of consultation before committing anything from this project to production. Over 80 per cent of Volvo's cars were being exported by the end of the 1970s, especially to the USA, so American consumers were asked for their opinions on the exterior and interior designs – and still the 700 series went into production! It must rank as one of the most controversial car designs ever to reach the showrooms, being almost universally slated by press and public alike for its sharp-edged styling.

But with looks being purely subjective (even if everybody was agreed the car was ugly), there would be no denying that it was well built. Prototype testing was exhaustive, with brake testing in the Alps, winter performance trials in Sweden and Canada and summer testing in the Australian Outback. Even then the testing didn't stop as 1,000 pre-production cars were then given to employees to rack up high mileages before they were recalled, inspected and scrapped.

After all this development work it was finally time for the car to go on sale, initially only in 760 GLE saloon form. Having invested so much time and money in its new car Volvo was definitely going to introduce the new range with a fanfare, so it was

There wasn't much choice at first, but it didn't take long for a whole range of petrol and diesel powerplants to become available.

decided to launch the car simultaneously in nine different countries. That meant 1,500 cars had to be built and transported globally in the utmost secrecy, but in February 1982, the 760 was shown publicly for the first time.

The initial reaction was mixed, with many commentators deciding very quickly that the styling was already very dated. Indeed, when *Autocar* asked Gordon Murray what he thought of the 760, he replied: 'To me that is obscene. That goes right against the grain and against everything everybody else is trying to do. To me it looks like a European version of an American car – a definite step backwards. If you look at the power the engine produces and the top speed of the car against the Rover 2600 or 3500 you'll see immediately how efficient it is at carrying four or five people along. In this day and age I would not like to believe it possible to produce something like that'.

As well as finding its square lines off-putting, many people thought it was too big, although it was actually the same size as the 240, albeit with a significantly longer wheelbase (109in against 104in), while also being shorter, lower and lighter than the 260. Although Volvo did not have much of a reputation for producing drivers' cars at that time, the company had tried very hard with the suspension to make sure the car wasn't criticised for handling badly. Although the front suspension was MacPherson strut, the rear suspension was completely new and was developed especially for the 700 series. The aim was to ensure that even when the car was being cornered hard, the rear track would stay constant regardless of loading on the wheels. The result was an axle supported by a sub-frame, which ensured predictable handling while also improving refinement levels.

All this work paid off, because although most of those who reviewed

the 760 reckoned that the styling wasn't nearly imaginative enough, at least the car was good to drive. American magazine *Car & Driver* tested the 760 on its launch and admitted that the car's styling would always be much more palatable to trans-Atlantic buyers than to European ones, due in no small part to it being heavily inspired by US design themes. Even then, it was no beauty and with poor aerodynamics it didn't take much to work out that Volvo was relying heavily on its name to sell its new car. But *Road & Track* was kinder to the 760, reckoning that although it wasn't especially attractive, it was good to drive. They even singled out the live rear axle as being better than many independent systems because Volvo had taken the

In 1984 the more-affordable 700 series went on sale, in the shape of the 740. Prices were much lower, but so were equipment levels.

The 780

In the same year that the Volvo 700 series estate was launched, there was another big debut for the range – that of the 780 on the Bertone stand at the 1985 Geneva Motor Show. Right through production the 700 series cars in estate and saloon forms were boxy and bland, but with Bertone's two-door version there was finally a derivative which was tasteful and elegant if a little angular.

Based on the 760 GLE, not a single panel was shared between the two-door car and the models produced by Volvo, although little was changed in underpinnings. The car was designed to be a range topper, equipped with everything from leather trim to air conditioning and a turbocharged version of the 2.5-litre V6 engine. In reality most cars sold were fitted with either diesel engines or four-cylinder petrol units, in both instances, aided by a turbocharger.

When it was introduced, the plan was to build the car for American and Italian markets only, with production limited to 2,500 units a year. Italian cars would get a 129bhp 2.4-litre six-cylinder turbo diesel while US cars would be powered by a 163bhp 2,458cc turbocharged petrol V6. Cooling problems with this engine led to American-market cars being fitted with the 2,849cc V6 powerplant under the bonnet instead.

With a price of around $35,000, the 780 was certainly exclusive, but with annual production limited to 4,000 cars between Europe and America, Bertone did not feel that sales would be so low that cars would end up being stockpiled. In the event, this number of cars in a single year was to prove optimistic, as during a production run which spanned from 1985 to 1990, just 8,518 examples were manufactured.

The 780 is more of a two-door saloon than a true coupé, but it is far more graceful than the 262C of the late 1970s, which was its true ancestor.

Throughout its lifetime, the 780 was Volvo's flagship. To reflect this, the interior was lavishly trimmed with leather and wood, while equipment levels were suitably high.

Prestige marques such as Jaguar, BMW and Mercedes were the main rivals to the 700 series, and the car's advertising reflected that.

time to engineer it properly so that the roadholding and handling were as good as the ride.

Predictably, safety was high on the agenda, with crumple zones, a safety cage, an isolated fuel tank and all manner of interior details to ensure passengers weren't injured in a collision. By this stage Volvo also had a good name for comfort as well as safety, so orthopaedically designed seats were standard and all the controls were developed with ergonomics in mind, ahead of aesthetics. The icing on the cake

was that equipment which rival manufacturers charged extra for was standard on the 760 – items such as electric windows, an electric sunroof, central locking and power steering were all included. So with good roadholding, high equipment levels, comfort and safety all part of the 760 ownership package, it wasn't difficult to look beyond the exterior design to see a reason for buying the car.

From the outset there were three engines available, including the familiar 2.8-litre B28E unit that had already been used in the 264 and 265. These cars were superseded by the 760, although a few final cars were made for export. With fuel injection the V6 powerplant developed 156bhp and 174lb ft, which was enough to propel the

Volvo from a standing start to 60mph (96kph) in 10 seconds and on to a top speed of 115mph (185kph). Selling alongside this was a 2.4-litre six-cylinder turbo diesel, known as the TD24 unit and which was sourced from Volkswagen. With 109bhp and 151lb ft of torque the car's performance wasn't very far behind that of the petrol-engined car and refinement levels were good. The final engine choice was a development of the 2.3-litre engine seen in the 240. Dubbed the B23ET, this turbocharged and intercooled four-cylinder petrol unit developed 173bhp, 0–62mph time of just 8.3 seconds and a top speed of 124mph (200kph).

As soon as the car was available for testing, *Car* magazine comprehensively evaluated one and

was unequivocal with its verdict –
'this is a damn good car which
is let down by its looks'. It handled
well, was spacious and comfortable,
was well equipped and was blessed
with good performance. In *Car's*
report it was also mentioned that
the 240 series would be pensioned
off within two years, but because
in fact it soldiered on for more
than a decade, and because the
760 cost significantly more than the
240, it made sense to introduce
something between the two. The
result was the 740, which arrived in
the spring of 1984. Prices were lower
because equipment levels were
rather less generous, although
buyers could specify enough
extras to take the car up to 760
spec if they wanted to – something
that made little sense as it would
have been more rational to simply

buy a 760 in the first place,
complete with a higher states of
engine tune. Transmission choices
were the same whichever car
was chosen, which meant a four-
speed plus overdrive manual
gearbox, or a three-speed-plus-
overdrive automatic.

Any doubts of the success of the
700 series, either during the
development process or following the
launch, had been dispelled by the
end of 1984. In 1983, the car's first
full year of sales, the 760 accounted
for 12 per cent of cars sold by the
Volvo. This figure rose much higher
the following year and it was clear
that offering owners of the most
expensive 240s and 260s an
alternative to a Mercedes or BMW
was just what had been needed.
Despite their satisfaction with Volvo's
products, when they wanted to

This is the car with which it seemed
Volvo could do no wrong – the 700
series estate. Apparently loved by
everyone, it had no true rivals thanks
to its combination of luxury and
carrying capacity.

upgrade to something more luxurious
and exclusive they had no alternative
but to switch allegiances – now they
could stay with Volvo. The result was
that 1983 saw 195,000 cars produced
at Volvo's main factory at Torslanda,
and when a new body plant was
opened in 1984 the quantity
produced again increased
considerably. Built to coincide with
the plant's 20th anniversary, nearly
100 robots had been installed to
speed up assembly.

This extra capacity was to prove
essential when the next version of the

Special-bodied cars

Companies such as Avon and Woodall-Nicholson offered limousine and hearse versions of the 700 series, with the Avon being available in various limousine forms. For around £20,000 there was a car stretched by 11.8in (30cm) while for £24,995 it was possible to specify a six-door example, with either 23.6in (60cm) or 35.4in (90cm) added to the car's length.

As well as independent coachbuilders producing their own limousines based on the 700 series, Volvo officially sanctioned limousines built by Yngve Nilssons Karosserifabrik. Based in Laholm in Sweden, Nilssons built cars based on both the saloon and estate bodyshells, the first of which had been produced as far back as 1975 using the 245 as a basis.

The more usual conversion was the production of a stretched estate with three rows of seats, the model being aimed at airport work for shuttling passengers and their luggage. Called the 245T (for Transfer) the range was expanded with an ambulance version as well as a hearse.

The introduction of the 700 series and subsequently the 900 series continued this arrangement and with the option of a stretched four-door or a six-door model there was no shortage of choice – and by out-sourcing the production, Volvo did not have to worry about building tiny numbers of special cars while still maintaining a profit. Not only that, but it could support buyers of such cars as well as ensuring that standards of production were maintained by being involved in the commissioning process.

Some of these special cars were little more than standard cars with bespoke fittings while others were barely recognisable as Volvos.

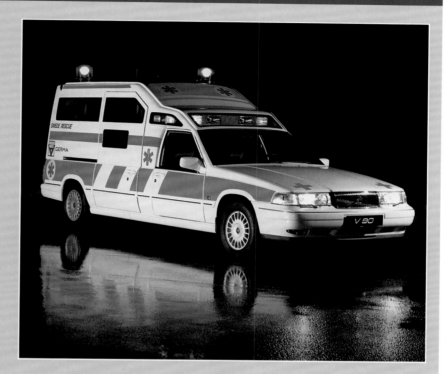

The 940 van is a classic case of the former – it even retains all the windows and doors of the standard estate – while the V90-based ambulance retains very little behind the B-post that an owner of the standard car would recognise.

Other popular conversions for the big Volvos include police-spec cars

Two conversions that show Volvo's flexibility: A V90 ambulance and an S80 limousine.

along with six-door or four-door stretched limousines and even armoured cars for VIPs who needed to be protected while on the move.

The 700 series was finally discontinued in 1990, and this is one of the last 760s made, which was built for the UK.

700 series was launched in 1985 – the estate. Such a move was completely expected, with estate versions of the 240 having proved so popular – nearly a third of sales globally were down to the estate and in Britain fewer than half the 240s sold had been saloons. When the concept version of the 700 series (the Volvo Concept Car) had been shown in 1980, it was an estate which was displayed. Initially, the new version of the 760 was only to be sold in North America, so it was no surprise that the car was launched at the Chicago Auto Show in February 1985.

That year's models also featured a couple of innovative features which

would not appear on rival cars for several years. The first of these was the traction control system, which was available as an option on the 760 Turbo. Using sensors to detect the (driven) rear wheels rotating faster than the front wheels, if the car started to suffer from wheelspin the fuel supply would be throttled to bring the car back under control. Also available as an option on the 760 Turbo was an anti-lock braking system, to ensure drivers didn't lose control of the car under emergency braking. Although Mercedes had been experimenting with electronic anti-lock brakes as far back as the early 1970s and had even offered them as an option on the S-class of 1978 it was some time before ABS would be commonplace.

The innovations continued in 1987 with the launch of a multi-link independent rear suspension for

saloon models, using coil springs with semi-trailing arms. Other car makers would begin shouting about their own designs of multi-link suspension soon after (notably Mercedes with its 190), but Volvo was the first to introduce the system on a mass-production car. The estate retained its coil-sprung live axle with trailing arms and Panhard rod, because the multi-link design would have compromised the car's load-carrying qualities. At the same time as the new suspension arrived, the 760 also received a facelifted nose to distinguish it from its cheaper brother. With a shallower grille, larger wipers which were concealed by an upswept bonnet and wider headlamps which incorporated driving lights, the changes were subtle, but effective.

In 1989, an effort was made to add a bit of spice to the range for its

final year, with the introduction of the B204GT engine for the 740. Featuring a turbocharger and intercooler, this highly tuned 2-litre 16-valve powerplant generated 200bhp at 5,300rpm, which was enough to make the 740, when so-equipped, the fastest production Volvo ever produced. If the 2.3-litre engine had been used – and tuned as highly – the performance would have been even more impressive but the concern was that perhaps there would have been more power than the gearbox could reliably cope with. Although Volvo was keen to improve its standing with car enthusiasts it certainly wasn't prepared to compromise on reliability. The result of the turbocharged engine in the 740 was a car that offered pretty explosive performance, with a top speed of 133mph (214kph) and the ability to

cover the 0–62mph sprint in just under eight seconds – which put it comfortably ahead of rivals such as the Audi 100 and Mercedes 230. It didn't allow it to match such icons as the Ferrari Testarossa and Lamborghini Countach though, which Volvo compared with the 740 in its American advertising. One advert featured the 740 Turbo alongside a Testarossa with the strapline: 'Until Ferrari builds a wagon, this is it'. Another advert had a 740 Turbo sitting beside a Countach with a trailer on the back. The heading along the top was:
'The basic idea behind the Volvo Turbo Wagon'.

Production of the 740 and 760 range ended in 1990, when the cars were replaced by the 940 and 960 respectively, but these were not all-new cars as they were based heavily on their predecessors and featured

Saloon models of the 700 series received a multi-link rear suspension in 1988. The 760's nose was also facelifted, although that of the 740 wasn't.

few significant changes. The most obvious improvement was in the styling, which had been softened at both ends so that the car looked more contemporary. Once again however, as has so often been the case with Volvos, the biggest change, at least for the 960, was under the bonnet. This brought the option of a 2,922cc six-cylinder powerplant which was not only the most powerful engine ever produced by Volvo for any of its cars, but it also signalled the demise of the PRV engine in Volvo's line-up. With double overhead camshafts

It's not difficult to see that the 940 is heavily based on its predecessor, the 740. In fact, apart from styling updates, there were relatively few differences between the four models.

operating four valves for each cylinder, the B6304F engine was available only with automatic transmission although smaller engines were still available with a manual gearbox.

No diesel versions of the 960 were offered because this was a premium model for high-fliers who could afford to feed the car's 20mpg (14 litres/100km) thirst. In the end it was only the engine and transmission (an extremely smooth unit developed by

Aisin-Warner and seen in the Lexus LS400) which prevented the car from being panned by car reviewers. The 700 series may have been a good car when it was launched in 1982, but by 1990 its basic underpinnings just weren't good enough for it to rival the very sophisticated competition it faced.

At least the 960 had a promising engine, but the 940, which was outwardly identical to the 960, used the 2.3-litre engine that had been used in the 740. The 940 also used the same beam rear axle that had featured on its predecessor, whereas the 960 was equipped with the 760's multi-link rear, as before – except an estate versions.

In total, the 900 series was in production for eight years, from 1990

until 1998. In that time there was almost no development of the car, the most significant change being the adoption of Volvo's patented SIPS (Side Impact Protection System) at the end of 1991. For some inexplicable reason the 960 was renamed in 1996, but not the 940, the 960 saloons becoming known as the S90 while estate versions carried V90 badges. The end of production of the 900 series was a significant step for Volvo, because it marked the end of the boxy big saloon for which the company had become famous. Instead, a new generation of luxury cars would arrive, bringing softer lines and excellent dynamics while retaining all the marque's safety credentials. At last, drivers would no longer have to justify their ownership of a Volvo.

The 960 had an excellent new 3.0-litre engine and much-improved suspension to distance itself from the 760 on which it was based.

Although the 960 was little more than an updated 760, the interior and dash were far more inviting on the later car.

The 400 *series*

Stealing an idea from an earlier photo opportunity with the 240 series, Volvo put a balloon in this shot with a 480ES, but somehow, it just didn't work.

Since the demise of the 1800ES, Volvo's image had moved sharply away from being a manufacturer of stylish and dependable cars to one which produced vehicles that were reliable, but dull. The problem was that people judged Volvo's cars before driving them – those who sampled them generally rather liked them.

480ES

1985–1995

ENGINE:

Four cylinders in line, iron block and alloy head	
Bore x stroke	81mm x 83.5mm
Capacity	1,721cc
Valvegear	Single overhead cam
Compression ratio	10.1:1
Fuelling	Renix multi-point fuel-injection
Maximum power	106bhp (ECE) at 5,500rpm
Maximum torque	108lb ft at 3,900rpm

TRANSMISSION:

Front-wheel-drive	
Five-speed manual or four-speed auto	
Final drive ratio:	4.067:1

SUSPENSION:

Front: Independent with MacPherson struts and wishbones
Rear: Beam axle with coil springs, dampers, longitudinal Watts linkages and single Panhard rod

STEERING:

Power-assisted rack-and-pinion	
Turns lock-to-lock	3.12

BRAKES:

Front & Rear:	Disc

WHEELS/TYRES:

5.5 x 14in alloy wheels with 185/60 HR 14 tyres

BODYWORK:

Three-door estate with unitary construction

DIMENSIONS:

Length	13ft 11in (4.23m)
Wheelbase	8ft 2½in (2.5m)
Track	4ft 7½in (1.41m)
Width	5ft 7in (1.71m)
Height	4ft 4in (1.32m)

WEIGHT:

	2,254lb (1,020kg)

PERFORMANCE: (Source: *Autocar*)

Max speed	110mph
0–60mph	10.3sec
30–50mph in top	14.3sec
50–70mph in top	14.2sec

UK PRICE WHEN NEW (June 1987):

Three-door hatch	£11,115

NUMBER MADE:

480ES	76,375
440	384,682
460	238,401

480ES

1992–1995

As 480 1.7 except:

ENGINE:

Bore x stroke	82.7mm x 93mm
Capacity	1,998cc
Valvegear	Single overhead cam
Compression ratio	9.81
Fuelling	Fuel injection
Maximum power	110bhp (ECE) at 5,500rpm
Maximum torque	123lb ft at 3,500rpm

480ES

Turbo

As 480ES except:

ENGINE:

Garrett AiResearch turbo fitted	
Compression ratio	8.11
Maximum power	120bhp (ECE) at 5,400rpm
Maximum torque	131lb ft at 3,300rpm

BRAKES:

Anti-lock brakes fitted as standard

WEIGHT:

	2,983lb (1,040kg)

PERFORMANCE: (Source: *Autocar* & *Motor*)

Max speed	123mph
0–60mph	8.6sec
30–50mph in top	11.7sec
50–70mph in top	10.2sec

UK PRICE WHEN NEW (July 1989):

Three-door hatch	£15,235

Something was needed to inject a bit of excitement into the range – the answer was the Dutch-built 480ES, which attempted to put some glamour back into the Volvo name, but it also failed to capture the imagination in anything like the way Volvo's previous sports hatch had managed. The use of a three-door estate configuration was no coincidence and pop-up headlamps were an attempt at making the 480ES look a bit sporty – unfortunately they were a bit passé by the time the car made its debut in 1985.

The car was initially proposed for the American market, as dealers there had asked for a sports car to stimulate interest in the rest of the Volvo range. In the event the car was not sold in the USA at all, a victim of exchange rates which meant the car

would not have made the company any money.

Underneath the skin the engineering was pretty conventional, although the 480ES did mark a significant departure for Volvo in that it was the first time the company had produced a front-wheel drive car. Coil and wishbone front suspension was used, with a simple coil-sprung dead axle at the rear – nothing hugely advanced, but the overall result was satisfactory with an acceptable balance between ride and handling.

Powering the 480ES was the same four-cylinder 1,721cc engine that you would find under the bonnet of a Renault 11, complete with Renix fuel-injection and 109bhp. The car was no ball of fire, but when *Car* magazine tested it, they were largely positive.

'The cabin of a 480 is not the place to get your kicks. But if it's a sense of comfortable well-being you seek, then this could be the car' they wrote. So it was generally agreed that the handling was good and the car was practical, but it did not have the style that the 1800 had exuded a quarter of a century before. And, just like the 1800, build quality wasn't up to scratch with electrical faults especially common and all sorts of troubles with the large frameless rear window cracking. When *Autocar* undertook its first test of a 480ES in the summer of 1987 its testers nearly ended up being involved in an accident when the steering lock broke and jammed the steering. Having lost the steering on public roads while travelling in traffic, not once but twice, *Autocar* reported it on the

The 480's dash was angular and functional, which was just what buyers expected from Volvo and – as they also expected – it worked very well.

magazine's opening page, and such reports did little to bolster confidence in the new model. If this was the vehicle that was to take Volvo in a new direction, some quick development needed to be undertaken if it wasn't to be a road to nowhere.

Eighteen months into production it was decided that strapping a Garrett AiResearch turbocharger to the engine would be a good idea to spice things up a bit. The result was 120bhp and a fine, if somewhat unrefined, performer. The Volvo was also expensive and build

quality still wasn't on a par with major rivals such as the BMW 320i and Saab 900 Turbo – which cost at least £1,000 less. Additionally, the difference in power was not as great as it could have been: after all, a power hike from 109bhp to 120bhp was not going to transform the car, and the chassis would have been able to handle significantly more power quite happily, but would Volvo buyers use the extra performance anyway? After all, those who purchased the 480 were probably buying into the Volvo reputation of looking after them while still seeing

Above: After years of producing cars such as the 200 series and 700 series (both of which were still in production at the time), the arrival of something as daring as the 480ES was quite a shock.

Below: Being a replacement for the 340 meant views were coloured before anybody had even driven the 440. Needless to say, the car suffered from prejudice from the outset.

The addition of a booted car for the 400 range did little to increase the car's standing in the eyes of reviewers, but the range still enjoyed a strong following thanks to its traditional Volvo virtues.

the model as something very stylish and atypical of the company.

Despite two years in which to iron out the faults before the Turbo arrived, there were still problems in the autumn of 1989 with engines running erratically, clutch cables wearing out quickly and all sorts of electrical maladies. The car may have been fun to drive, but if it wasn't dependable it wouldn't be taken seriously by the motoring press or the buying public. In the spring of 1992, all but the base

model of the 480ES range received a 1,998cc version of the B20F engine, in a bid to improve performance, but by this stage the motoring press had lost interest in the car. As a result the 480 received no coverage at all in the mainstream car magazines between 1990 and 1995, when the car was taken out of production, ensuring it was firmly out of the eyes of the buying public. When Richard Bremner reviewed the 480ES for *Car* magazine, on its demise in 1995, he made reference to its decent power combined with low weight: 'This meant there was some danger of a sporty steer – pretty radical from a company that considered having fun at the wheel as acceptable as seducing a nun'. Faint praise indeed, especially when taken with Bremner's parting line: 'Good grief, it's a Volvo worth preserving. And there aren't many of them.'

Volvo's investment in this small front-wheel drive platform would have made no sense if it had just been for the 480ES, which would never be anything more than a niche car. From the day it was first shown it was entirely predictable that a new small hatchback – and probably a saloon – would follow. After all, the 340 and 360 were positively ancient by the time the 480ES made its debut, so the launch of something new was well overdue, but it was to take another three years from the introduction of the 480ES before a new small car from Volvo was to go on sale. That car was the 440, shown to the world's press in June 1988 and available in GL, GLT and Turbo versions. Following the almost universally reviled (at least by the motoring press) 340 and 360, it was no surprise that the 400 series got a hard time almost immediately, thanks to its completely unadventurous styling as well as its ten-a-penny engineering. Britain had proved to be the biggest export market for the 300 series, so if anything, that showed that car buyers didn't care too much about what they were told by so-called experts – which was just as well for Volvo!

A four-door version of the 400 series was launched in 1989. The development of 460, as the new model was called, mirrored that of the five-door, which meant that at first just a 1.7-litre engine was offered, the unit being the Renault 1,721cc four-cylinder powerplant that had been fitted to the 340. By 1991 a 1,794cc petrol engine had joined the range and by 1994 the entry-level car was fitted with a

The factory convertible

The convertible version of the 480ES was two years old before it even had its first public showing. After the Dutch arm of Volvo announced in the summer of 1987 that a drop-top 480 would be going on sale, the parent company scuppered plans to move swiftly with the project. There were concerns that the car would not live up to the safety standards required of a Volvo, so although the car was scheduled to debut at the 1987 Amsterdam Motor Show, it was not actually seen by the public until the 1990 Geneva Motor Show.

Developed by the American Sunroof Company, the 480ES convertible aroused considerable interest when it was shown, but would Volvo build it or was it just another project that would never get off the ground? Although the car received a lot of bodyshell stiffening, there were still reservations about how well its occupants would be protected in the event of a roll-over.

By 1989, Brussels-based EBS had developed the car further and an announcement was made that by the beginning of 1991 the car would be available at the rate of between 1,000 and 2,000 each year. When Renault tried to work with EBS on a convertible version of its R5 and the deal turned sour, Volvo became very wary about working with such a company, so the project stagnated.

The next stop was UK company Motor Panels, which continued to work on the car and by early 1990 another announcement was made that the convertible 480 would be on sale before the year was out, with around 1,200 examples to be produced annually in Holland. By this stage there was a fixed roll bar and the rear seats had been ditched so that the car was strictly a two-seater, but all this work came to nothing because in the end, the convertible 480 did not reach production, the victim of an over-long gestation process.

1596cc engine developing 82bhp. From 1989, a catalytic converter was available as a no-cost option on most derivatives and because diesel engines were beginning to get very popular by the early 1990s, in 1994 a 1.9-litre turbo diesel joined the range.

By 1995, Volvo was revisiting its past by offering a continuously variable transmission – ever since the 343 had been offered with a conventional manual gearbox the company had seemed keen to forget about its experimentation with oddball transmissions which buyers did not trust. However, more than a decade after it seemed the Variomatic had been consigned to the history books, manufacturers such as Ford and Nissan were trying

out new versions of the CVT. Volvo decided to have another go and sure enough the car disappeared without trace almost as quickly as it appeared. When the *Top Gear* TV programme got its hands on a 1.8-litre version in the summer of 1995 it went so far as to say the 440 was quite an acceptable car, but that with a normal manual gearbox it would be much better. Sure enough, buyers stayed away and the CVT system once more disappeared from the options list.

Despite the fact that the 440 and 460 were invisible cars as far as the motoring press were concerned, they soldiered on, selling in reasonable numbers until they were replaced by the S40 and V40, which arrived in 1995 and 1996 respectively.

Volvo *in the* 1990s – *and beyond*

This was the car that turned things round for Volvo. The 850 in Turbo form was far better to drive than to look at, although the edges were rounded off slightly.

Although the introduction of the 850 in 1992 did not appear especially significant to the casual observer, it marked a new path for Volvo. Not only was it the first of a new generation of slightly more rounded-looking models, but great attention had been paid to the car's dynamics, with completely new delta-link rear suspension endowing the car with handling equal to the best of its competitors. It also featured front-wheel drive, which was not only unusual for a Volvo (although the 400 series had offered this since 1985),

850 GLT

1992–1996

ENGINE:

Four cylinders in line, alloy block and head	
Bore x stroke	83mm x 90mm
Capacity	2,435cc
Valvegear	Double overhead camshaft
Compression ratio	10.5:1
Fuelling	Bosch Jetronic multi-point fuel injection
Maximum power	170bhp (DIN) at 6,200rpm
Maximum torque	162lb ft at 3,300rpm

TRANSMISSION:

Rear-wheel-drive	
Five-speed manual, four-speed automatic	
Final drive ratio	4.00:1 (without overdrive)

SUSPENSION:

Front: Struts, coil springs, lower wishbones, anti-roll bar
Rear: Semi-independent with delta-link axles, longitudinal trailing arms, coil springs, anti-roll bar

STEERING:

Power assisted rack-and-pinion	
Turns lock-to-lock	3.2

BRAKES:

Front & Rear:	Discs
Servo-assisted with anti-lock brakes	

WHEELS/TYRES:

6.5 x 15in wheels with 195/60 VR15 tyres

BODYWORK:

All-steel monocoque
Four-door saloon, five-door estate from 1993

DIMENSIONS:

Length	15ft 3in (4.66m)
Wheelbase	8ft 9in (2.67m)
Track	5ft 0in (1.52m)
Width	5ft 9in (1.76m)
Height	4ft 7in (1.40m)

WEIGHT: 3,174lb (1,443kg)

PERFORMANCE: (Source: *Autocar*)

Max speed	127mph
0–60mph	9.7sec
30–50mph in top	3.6sec
50–70mph in top	5.0sec

UK PRICE WHEN NEW (November 1992)

Four-door saloon	£21,795

NUMBER MADE:

850 saloon	390,727
850 estate	326,703

The Renault partnership

By the end of the 1970s it was clear to Volvo that it could not afford to continue to develop its cars without some outside financial assistance. The answer proved to be an alliance with Renault, which was announced on 19 December 1979. Under the terms of the deal Renault would acquire 10 per cent of Volvo for SKr330m with an option of increasing its shareholding from first 15 then to 20 per cent.

In the event, Renault exercised its option to increase its stake to 15 per cent in 1981, but once things had started to pick up for Volvo the decision was made to buy back all but 9.4 per cent of the shares in 1983, with the rest of the shares being purchased the following year.

This wasn't the end for Renault and Volvo in terms of a partnership, as on 23 February 1990 the announcement was made that the two companies were to merge. This was the biggest news story ever to hit the Swedish motor industry and it was clear that Volvo's shareholders were not going to take it lying down. Initially, Volvo's shares increased in value as the news was greeted positively, but this very quickly changed once it became obvious that Volvo was really being swallowed up by the French car manufacturer. Volvo claimed it could save SKr25 billion over the next decade, but nothing happened until September 1993.

Since the announcement had first been made that the two companies were to form an alliance, Volvo had done badly while Renault had done well in the marketplace. Volvo had been forced to enter into a round of cost-cutting measures because of major losses – the company posted its first loss since 1929, which was just two years after it had been formed. Declining sales and falling exchange rates now led to enforced early retirements, redundancies and other measures that would hopefully shore up Volvo's finances. Meanwhile, Renault's sales remained fairly buoyant and by 2 December 1993 things came to a head, and a board meeting was called which would settle the matter for good. It was clear that not only were most of the Volvo's shareholders against a merger, but so were most of the company's top managers. The result was the mass resignation of Volvo President Pehr Gyllenhammar and the entire board.

In estate form, the 850 Turbo was unbeatable. It offered everything including safety, performance, a great driving experience and amazing practicality – no wonder they're still highly sought after today.

Thoroughly modern, but still clearly a Volvo. The 850's dash is square and slabby, but is well laid out and comprehensively equipped.

but it was also very unusual for the class – high power outputs were common in this size of car and the best end through which to channel lots of power is not necessarily the front. Indeed, by the time the 850 T5-R made its appearance in 1994 it was providing 250bhp to the front wheels, something which did not do its tyres any favours. It was the 850GLT which single-handedly began to turn round the image of Volvo because although it was still pretty boxy by anybody's standards, this was the model that showed dynamics were no longer unimportant to the company.

The marketing campaign constructed around the 850 focused on dynamics ahead of everything else – including safety. Yet while any seriously powerful car would always have rear-wheel drive, here was an executive performance car which was rapid, surefooted and handled well, providing the excellent

Until 1996, Volvo hadn't put a four-wheel-drive car into production. The 850 AWD was launched in that year to compete with other 'lifestyle estates' which were becoming increasingly popular.

Peter Horbury

Volvo had never embraced the concept of built-in obsolescence. Jaw-dropping looks had never been important either, but by the middle of the 1980s it was obvious that the world had changed since the days when a car could be designed with a ruler and still sell in profitable numbers. Jan Wilsgaard had retired and a successor was required – which was Peter Horbury's cue to take on the role of head of design for Volvo. It's this unassuming man who has single-handedly turned round the design of Volvo's products, moving away from angular boxes to curvy, desirable shapes.

Having graduated from the Royal College of Art in 1974, with a Masters degree in automotive design, Horbury initially worked for Chrysler – which had sponsored him

throughout his degree. In 1977, he moved to Ford where he stayed for two years before moving to Volvo as a consultant designer. By 1986, he had been appointed director of styling and design at MGA Developments before he moved to Volvo to become design director in 1991. Having successfully turned round Volvo's image Horbury was promoted to become head of design for the Premier Automotive Group, which comprises the most aspirational marques in Ford's portfolio. Alongside Volvo that means Horbury now has a hand in the designs of Land Rover, Aston Martin and Jaguar.

Peter Horbury is responsible for turning round the design of Volvo, although the company's chassis engineers must take a lot of credit for making the cars truly desirable.

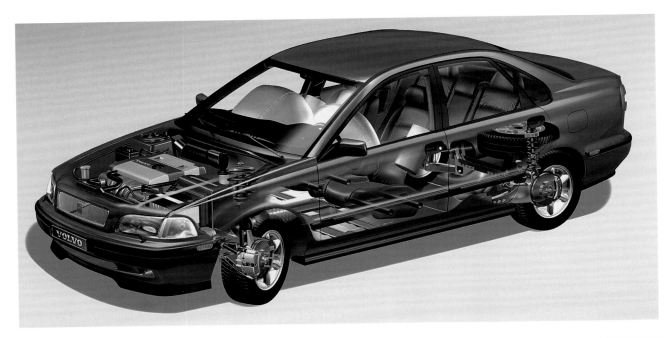

Opposite: The launch of the S40 wasn't a high spot, because the car was so mediocre at everything it did. Even a couple of facelifts failed to raise it above the position of 'also-ran'.

Opposite, below: At least the V40 had practicality on its side, and in a crash it would look after its occupants well. But dynamically, it was so unexceptional that it only sold because it displayed a Volvo badge.

Right: With the demise of the C70 coupé, the C70 convertible has been left to fly the sporting flag. It is more of a cruiser than a hot-rod, unless the T5 engine is under the bonnet . . .

Below: The Volvo S90 and V90.

The Mitsubishi partnership

In the early 1990s, Volvo found itself looking for a company with which it could develop a new small car to replace the 400 series. That company turned out to be Mitsubishi, and in conjunction with the Dutch government, a factory was set up in Born, in the Netherlands, to build a new range of small cars for the two companies. Volvo already had an alliance with the Dutch government going back to the late 1970s when Volvo had bought Dutch car maker Daf. The introduction of Mitsubishi into the plan meant there was more capital available to develop a car, and the NedCar name was chosen for the company which would facilitate this.

NedCar would develop and build cars for both Volvo and Mitsubishi while the two car makers would retain their own separate sales and marketing groups. By 1995, Volvo was producing its S40 alongside Mitsubishi's Carisma and by October 1997 a deal was in place for Volvo to market Mitsubishi's Canter light truck. When Mitsubishi introduced its GDI (gasoline direct injection) engine in 1997 the co-operation expanded with the fitting of the powerplant to the V40 and S40 from the following year. When the NedCar project had been set up the agreement had always been for the Dutch government to sell its stake in 1998, and as planned, Mitsubishi and Volvo bought the government's shareholding – at

about the same time as Ford was looking at buying Volvo.

Things progressed from there with the companies taking a stake in each other and the intention was to develop trucks and buses together. There was a fly in the ointment however, because Volvo's largest competitor, DaimlerChrysler, acquired a majority shareholding in Mitsubishi at the start of 2001. As a result, Volvo was obliged to sell its interest in Mitsubishi to Daimler-Chrysler in April that year and cut its ties with the Japanese company.

Mitsubishi had the Carisma and Volvo the 400 series. Both cars were as forgettable as each other, but they did well for their makers.

There was a four-wheel-drive version of the 850, but the introduction of the V70XC (for cross-country) marked a change of branding for Volvo, with the focus being on the lifestyle market.

The all-new V70 of 2000 retained its predecessor's name, although the new car was a huge leap forward, and consequently received one plaudit after another.

The bi-fuel cars

With the rocketing cost of fuel, many drivers were starting to convert their cars to run on LPG (liquid petroleum gas) by the early 1990s. By the end of that decade the trend had accelerated and the British government had even set up an agency (called Powershift) to encourage it. As the number of outlets selling the fuel increased it became viable for car makers to offer cars which would run on LPG without needing any conversion. Volvo was one of the first, with an LPG-powered version of its 850 on sale as early as 1996. From that car onwards, Volvo offered a dual-fuel (later bi-fuel) version of its largest cars and the S80 was engineered from the outset with a second fuel tank so that the car could attain European Whole Vehicle Approval status.

By the beginning of 2001, with LPG-powered cars becoming increasingly common, and it wasn't only the biggest cars in the range which were being offered with factory-fitted LPG fuel tanks – even the S40 and V40 were available as bi-fuel models. The rationale behind the move was to allow drivers to fill up their cars at half the cost of using petrol, while knowing that the engineering employed in the conversion was up to Volvo standards. By removing the spare wheel and fitting a second fuel tank to take the petrol, the main tank could be used for LPG. Then if one of the fuels ran out and (in the case of the LPG) was hard to find because of limited availability, the car could be run on petrol instead.

performance was a 2.5-litre engine which was a development of the unit seen in the 960, which continued to be sold alongside the 850 until 1996. Generating 170bhp, it was an all-alloy five-cylinder version of the six-pot seen in the 850's predecessor, complete with twin overhead camshafts and four valves for each cylinder. As well as this, a 2.0-litre version was offered and there were even two-valve versions available alongside a 225bhp 2.3-litre turbocharged unit – so nobody was going to be put off buying an 850 because of a lack of choice!

The result of all this effort on the part of Volvo certainly paid dividends. 'Anyone who doesn't know by now that Volvo has produced a real driver's car in the 850 must live on another planet. The arrival of this well-built, spacious, front-drive five-cylinder saloon with zestful performance and rewarding handling has been one of the most encouraging automotive stories of 1992' wrote *Autocar* of the 2.5-litre 850. In 1993, an estate version of the car went on sale, this marking the start of Volvo's move to vertically stacked rear-light clusters running down the sides of the tailgate. An extension of the high-level rear brake light idea which

Above: Introduced to compete head-on with other lifestyle four-wheel-drive estates such as the Audi AllRoad, the Cross Country is designed to take Volvo even further into this territory.

Opposite, above: It took a long time for Volvo to eradicate all traces of the 700 series from its range, but the launch of the S80 in 1998 marked a fresh start for the company's top models.

Opposite, below: Ever since the demise of the 240 series, Volvo had no medium-sized saloon to offer. The S60, which went on sale in Autumn 2000, changed all that. Seen here in racing livery, it struggled to compete with BMW's M3.

had been introduced to reduce rear-end impacts, this styling device has since become used throughout the car industry. Other than that there was little to distance the car from its saloon counterpart, sharing the same mechanicals, but with a choice of just the 2.5-litre five-cylinder engines or the 225bhp turbocharged 2.3-litre unit.

The next major step for Volvo was the introduction of its first four-wheel-drive production car.

Launched at the 1995 Geneva Motor Show, the 4WD 850 estate was not intended to be an off-roader – instead, it marked Volvo's attempt at making the car even safer by offering greater traction when driving conditions were less than ideal. It did not go into production until the spring of the following year, with the North American market the main focus for the car, but a four-wheel-drive could never be seen as anything more than just a niche model, and the really significant introduction for Volvo in 1995 was that of the S40. Launched at the Paris Motor Show, this was the car that would replace the 400 series,

although those cars continued to be built alongside the S40 in the Netherlands until the end of the following year. Under the skin the car shared much with Mitsubishi's new Carisma, and between them the S40, Carisma and V40 – introduced at the end of the year – would underwhelm the motoring press with their completely unexceptional dynamics.

Altogether more palatable was the introduction of the C70, which marked a welcome return for Volvo to the sports coupé market. First shown at the 1996 Paris Motor Show, the C70 was developed jointly by Volvo and Tom Walkinshaw Racing – the

company which had taken over the Arrows F1 team earlier that year and had acquired the services of reigning World Champion Damon Hill to drive for them. Not only that, but in conjunction with Porsche, TWR had won Le Mans that year, so there was certainly no lack of confidence in the company. Since the demise of the P1900 in 1957, Volvo had not offered a convertible in its range. In fact, with the exception of a few drophead 1800s and a single factory 480 convertible, this was a body style that was noticeable by its absence from the Volvo line-up. But that was all remedied with the launch at the 1997 Detroit Auto

It was barely on sale in mid-2003, but Volvo's SUV had already racked up plaudits everywhere – and as a result, the car was an immediate sell-out in many markets.

Show of the convertible C70. The choice of venue for the launch signalled very clearly that the North American market was the one for which the car had been developed, and once more, the work had been done by TWR. In the event, the convertible version of the C70 would outlive the closed car, with the latter version being taken out of production at the end of 2002 so as to focus on the more glamorous open-topped derivative.

For consistency across the range the big saloons and estates were renamed in 1996 (for the 1997 model year), when they became the S70 and V70 respectively. With 'S'

standing for saloon and 'V' for versatility, the main changes to the cars were cosmetic, with a new front end and revisions to the saloon's rear-end styling. By the time these cars were taken out of production in 2000 they were looking desperately long in the tooth, descended in their styling as they were from the 700 series which had been launched in 1982 – and which had been developed at the end of the 1970s. So the arrival of the S80 saloon in the summer of 1998 was just the ticket; an estate – confusingly retaining the V70 name – made its debut at the 2000 Detroit Auto Show.

The launch of this new executive

Volvo under Ford

Volvo's acquisition by an American company in 1999 was a move that had nearly happened 70 years before. In 1929, Volvo had yet to make a profit and its owner, SKF, was on the verge of giving up hope. SKF President Björn Prytz had begun talks with Charles Nash, head of America's giant Nash Corporation, with a view to selling the Swedish company. Charles Nash had already set sail to sign the deal when Assar Gabrielsson persuaded Prytz not to sell – Gabrielsson had to put forward SKr220,000 of his own money to secure the company's future.

The gamble paid off, as by September 1929 Volvo was operating at a profit. A slip into the red the following month was a blip and from November onwards the company stayed resolutely in the black – a position that would have been rather more appealing to Ford than the mass of red ink on the balance sheets when Nash had been approached seven decades earlier.

It was announced on 28 January 1999 that Volvo Cars would be bought by the Ford Motor Company, leaving the rest of the Volvo Group to manufacture trucks and buses. The price agreed for the sale was SKr50 billion ($6bn), a price which was reflected by Volvo's healthy, profit-making status. But despite this profitability, Volvo had become too small to be able to compete with the big manufacturers as it did not enjoy their economies of scale.

A shareholders' meeting on 8 March 1999 approved the takeover and that paved the way for Volvo to become one of the marques in Ford's Premier Automotive Group – along with Aston Martin, Jaguar, Lincoln and Land Rover.

contender from Volvo was the start of a new design direction. Peter Horbury's design team was moving away from straight lines to softer, more flowing curves and the results were instant – as soon as it was shown the company was viewed in a different light. 'This is one good-looking car. And it's a Volvo. Let the ramifications of that sink in and it's hard not to believe that the new S80 is perhaps the most revolutionary Volvo ever – a real mould-breaker' commented *Autocar*. And it was, because suddenly, drivers were no longer embarrassed to admit that the keys in their pocket were for a Volvo. With a choice of 2.4-litre, 2.9-litre or 2.8-litre bi-turbo petrol engines – along with the excellent five-cylinder diesel later on – there was something for everybody.

By the autumn of 2000 the final gap in the Volvo range was filled. With extra-large and medium estates and saloons available, all that was needed was something in between. For some reason Volvo decided that a mid-range estate was not something that it wanted to offer, so in the event just a four-door saloon arrived, wearing the S60 badge. The new arrival was a slightly smaller version of the S80 and at first there were

three turbocharged petrol engines. The base model featured a 180bhp 1,984cc unit while above that was a 200bhp 2,435cc powerplant – both with four-cylinders. Top of the range was the T5, with a monstrous 250bhp on tap from a blown 2,319cc five-cylinder engine, and just like the T4 versions of the S40 and V40, there was really far too much power going through the front wheels. In the dry it was quite fun, but in the wet the car really struggled to put the power down and it was all too easy to get through a set of tyres without really trying, just by exploiting the power on a regular basis.

Although the arrival of the S60 seemed to give Volvo a complete range, market trends meant the portfolio had a significant gap in it while an off-roader, or SUV (sport utility vehicle) was not offered. The ACC (Adventure Concept Car), which was first shown at the 2001 Detroit Auto Show gave a taster of what was to come a full two years before the car was available in production form, as the XC90. At the same time as Volvo's entry into the crowded SUV market there were other major manufacturers launching similar products, not least Porsche and Volkswagen with their Cayenne

and Touareg respectively. While those cars received mixed reviews – at least in terms of whether or not the marketplace really had room for them – the Volvo received an overwhelmingly positive reception.

So where does Volvo go from here, with compact, medium and large cars on offer, alongside a sporting convertible and an SUV? The answer would seem to be even further upmarket with strongly sporting versions of its cars from a new division of the company. Carrying the new R brand, the S60 R (which was first seen as the Performance Car Concept at the 2000 Paris Motor Show) and V70 R feature the most powerful engine yet to come from Volvo. With 300bhp, the 2.5-litre five-cylinder powerplant allows both cars to despatch the 0–62mph sprint in under six seconds. Volvo has listened to criticisms that its most powerful cars can't put the power down with front-wheel drive so these new cars feature four-wheel drive and what Volvo touts as Four-C technology – the continuously controlled chassis concept. This allows the car's computers to adjust the suspension and torque bias – among many other things – up to 500 times each second. It's all a far cry from the PV4 of 1927!

Index